nitty gritty books

No Salt, No Sugar, No Fat	Pasta & Rice	Cheese Guide & Cookbook
Fast and Delicious	Yogurt	Miller's German
Getting Started in the Kitchen	Cocktails & Hors d'Oeuvres	Quiche & Souffle
Brunch	Casseroles & Salads	To My Daughter With Love
My Cookbook	Food Processor Cookbook	Natural Foods
Family Favorites	Soups & Stews	Working Couples
Cookies	Crepes & Omelets	Mexican
Cooking for 1 or 2	Microwave Cooking	Fisherman's Wharf Cookbook
Chicken Cookery	Vegetable Cookbook	Barbecue Cookbook
Skillet Cookbook	Bread Baking	Ice Cream Cookbook
Convection Oven	The Crockery Pot Cookbook	Blender Cookbook
Household Hints	Classic Greek Cooking	The Wok, a Chinese Cookbook
Seafood Cookbook	Low Carbohydrate Cookbook	Fondue Cookbook
Quick Breads	Kid's Cookbook	

designed with giving in mind

Nitty Gritty Productions ● P.O. Box 5457 ● Concord, California 94524

To our Sons and Daughters with love.

GETTING STARTED
in the
KITCHEN

by

Jane Martin Giulieri
Carol Tuxbury Gribbon

Alice Rademacher Hoskins
Jean C. Langley

Sue Lundahl Campbell
Ruth Dathe French

illustrated by Mike Nelson

Nitty Gritty® Book*
Published by
Nitty Gritty® Productions
P.O. Box 5457
Concord, California

*Nitty Gritty® Books Trademark
Owned by Nitty Gritty® Productions
Concord, California

Printed in the U.S.A.
by Mariposa Press
Concord, California
Edited by Jackie Walsh

ISBN 0-91195-4-63-5
Library of Congress Catalog Card Number #81-81483

Table of Contents

HOW THIS BOOK CAME ABOUT...

We saw the need for a book of this kind as our children were "cutting the apron strings" and becoming independent. Some left for college or first apartments, others became new brides or grooms; each cheerfully carried away a few of our pots and pans, only to call home wistfully a few days later for some favorite recipes or a cooking hint or two.

Our active teenagers found themselves more involved with cooking to accommodate changing family patterns. For these young people cooking seemed a struggle which often interfered with their activities. They, too, asked for help.

We six (mothers, experienced cooks and home economists) realized we had taken basic cooking and food knowledge for granted. Looking back at our own first attempts in the kitchen, we gained a new appreciation for our own mothers' helpful roles. Thus, the idea for a handy, how-to guide for the person just "getting started in the kitchen" was born.

Our first step was to develop a questionnaire asking specifically what kitchen skills and recipes the young people wanted. When we tallied the results we found suggestions to keep things simple and uncomplicated. They wanted easy directions. Their need, they told us, was not for gourmet food, but for quick, easy adaptations of old favorites, usable on the campus hotplate or in the first-apartment oven, and geared to their time limitations as well as their dollar-wise budgets. Also important to them was basic kitchen and food know-how. Those starting out on their own requested a list of minimum cooking equipment that could be packed easily and transported safely in case they changed living quarters.

Second, we selected a simple assortment of cooking equipment without including any electrical appliances. This portable box of equipment can go anywhere and be stored even in the corner of a dorm room.

Third, we chose a variety of recipes from family favorites most often requested and adapted them to use the equipment in the box. We also considered the need for cooking small quantities.

Then our young adults and teenagers kitchen-tested both the recipes and preparation methods. They offered suggestions, ideas, and fresh insights which we welcomed and used. Husbands, too, helped by tasting the results, and giving their approval.

Putting it all on paper was our final step. Now you can tuck your copy in your equipment box and get started in your own kitchen.

Introduction

Hooray! You're on your own. Getting Started in the Kitchen is a cookbook written especially for you. Even if you can't boil water, you can and will survive.

The first step is gathering just enough equipment to cook healthful, tasty meals. The equipment we suggest is all that you need to prepare and serve the recipes in this book. Realizing that cost, storage space and ease of packing are important, we have kept the list simple. The entire collection fits neatly into a 12 x 18 x 12-inch box.

Next, it's necessary to understand a recipe and know a little about the kitchen. Not to worry. You will find all the information you need to cook our recipes, plus many extra tips included in this cookbook.

While the temptation to skip cooking altogether and go out for a quick bite may be great, you will put less strain on your pocketbook if you cook at home. Don't panic. We have taken special care with each recipe to eliminate guesswork and insure success. Each recipe is accompanied by a list of equipment used in its preparation. Directions are brief and easy to understand. Generally, the recipes are for two servings. If you plan on having company, it's a snap to double or triple a recipe.

Kitchen Staples

Every cook's list of absolute, basic, kitchen staples contains different items, but here are the ones we think most cooks will agree on.

Flour: all purpose and perhaps whole wheat
Sugar: white and brown
Vegetable oil
Salt and Pepper
Vinegar
Cereal and grains: rice, pasta and
    breakfast cereals
Baking powder
Baking soda
Coffee
Tea
Catsup, Mayonnaise, Mustard
Seasonings and Spices: minced dried onion,
    garlic powder, cinnamon, nutmeg,
    oregano, basil and vanilla

Other kitchen supplies:
    (non-food items)
    Diswashing Detergent
    Cleanser
    Sponge or dishcloth and dish towel
    Aluminum foil, plastic wrap,
        wax paper
    Paper towels
    Containers: empty food jars, coffee
        cans, plastic bags, juice cans

Equipment for Getting Started

It takes only the equipment listed on the next few pages to prepare the recipes in this cookbook. All the equipment can be packed and toted efficiently in a 12 x 18 x 12-inch box.

Collect or buy the best quality cooking equipment you can afford. Cost is not the only indication of quality. Bargains are available. Check the local paper. Look for garage sales. See what second-hand stores have to offer and don't overlook catalogs and department store sales.

One last tip: resist the urge to buy gadgets and small appliances until you've worked with the *Getting Started in the Kitchen Cookbook,* and can better judge your needs.

Essential Cooking Equipment

Dutch oven, with close fitting lid: 5-quart size, oven-proof
Frying pan: large, 10 inches, uses Dutch oven lid, oven-proof
Frying pan: small, 7 inches, non-stick, easy clean is convenient
Saucepan, with lid: 2-quart size
Double boiler insert: 5-cup size, uses saucepan lid, oven proof, fits in saucepan as double
   boiler
Pie pan: 9-inch
Baking pans: two, 8 inches square
Baking sheet: 12 x 15-1/2 inches, with sides

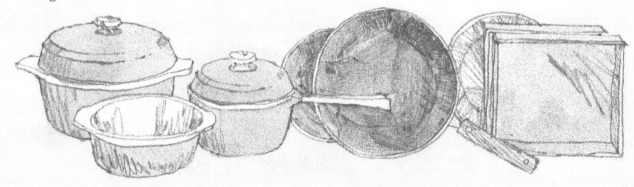

Mixing bowls: small, medium and large; large being 3-quart size, stainless steel is the best choice

Pitcher: 2-quart, with tight fitting lid

Loaf pans: two, 5 x 2 x 3 inches, oven-proof

Muffin pan: 6 compartments

Potholders: 2

Tip: buy oven-proof equipment so it can be used both on top of the range and in the oven. Double boiler insert makes a bowl and covered casserole too!

Essential Cooking Tools

Measuring cups: one set of 4, stainless steel is best
Measuring spoons: one set of 4, stainless steel is best
Vegetable peeler: stainless steel is best
Small knife: 4-inch blade
Large knife: 6 to 8-inch blade
Cooking fork: heat resistant
Slotted spoon: long handle, heat resistant

Mixing spoon: long handle, heat resistant
Spatula: metal
Rubber scraper
Beater: wire whisk or egg beater
Can openers: two, 1 for removing lids and 1 for punching holes
Cutting board: 12 x 16-inch, plastic is best
Grater: flat

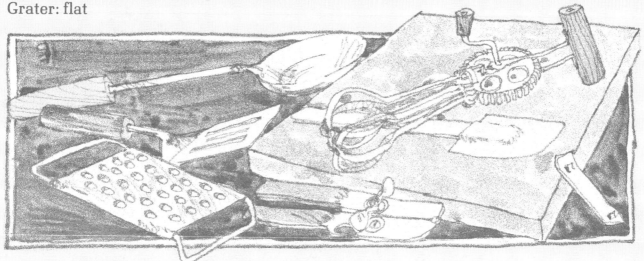

Non-Essential But Handy Equipment

Teakettle

Kitchen timer

Colander

Coffee pot

Corkscrew

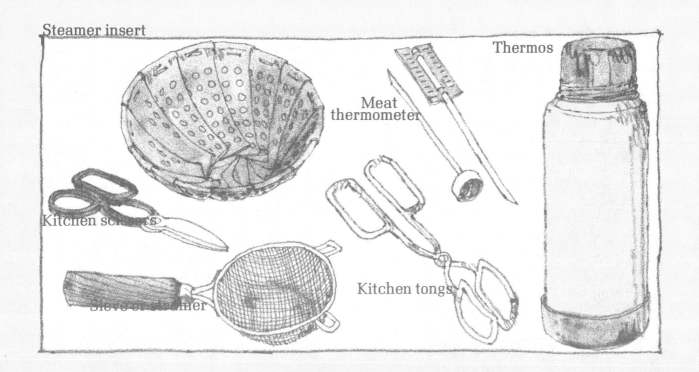

Steamer insert

Thermos

Meat thermometer

Kitchen scissors

Kitchen tongs

Sieve or strainer

11

Equipment Box

Box should measure at least 12 x 18 x 12 inches. Use any one of the following:

cardboard box
vegetable or fruit crate
ice chest
large canvas tote bag

laundry basket
large waste basket
suitcase, old or new

Tip: a covered container, sturdy enough to sit on, is most practial.

Dishes

You'll want at least two place settings of dishes and flatware. If space permits, four to eight may be more convienient. **Tip:** buy dinnerware that is oven-proof.

Dinner plates, 2
Cereal or Soup Bowls, 2
Mugs, large, 2
Glasses, 4 or more of 16-ounce size

Knives, 2
Forks, 2
Spoons, 2

Menu Planning

Use the Basic Four Food Group guide listed on the next page when planning your menus. It is the simplest way to make sure you get all the nutrients you need each day.

Keep in mind also, as you plan your menus, that color, texture and flavor combinations are very important too. Here are two examples of poor menu planning. The first meal consists of sauteed halibut, boiled potatoes, steamed cauliflower and vanilla pudding for dessert. All the foods are white. Not an appealing menu. To remedy it, substitute a vegetable with some color (green beans, sliced tomatoes or asparagus) for the potatoes and a salad for the cauliflower. The pudding could be perked up easily by spooning a little raspberry jam on top. Here's another unappetizing menu: creamed tuna, chopped spinach, mashed potatoes and ice cream. Perfect for after major dental surgery. A nice big salad and fresh rolls would be better than the spinach and mashed potatoes. For dessert, how about crisp lemon cookies?

Armed with the Basic Four Food Group and the facts in the previous paragraph, you should be well on your way to creating nutritionally sound and appealing menus.

Breads-Cereal

4 or more servings

Enriched or whole grain
Added milk improves
nutritional values

Veg.-Fruit

4 or more servings

Include dark green or
yellow vegetables,
citrus fruit or tomatoes

Meat Group

2 or more servings

Meats, fish, poultry, eggs, or
cheese—with dry beans
peas, nuts as alternates

Milk Group

3 or more glasses milk—Children
smaller glasses for some children under 8

4 or more glasses—Teenagers

2 or more glasses—Adults

Cheese, ice cream and other milk-made
foods can supply part of the milk

15

Kitchen Terms

Bake: cook in the oven

Beat: mix vigorously with a spoon or beaters

Boil: heat water or other liquid so hot that bubbles rise continuously to the surface; cook in a liquid that is boiling

Chop: cut into pieces (size is usually specified)

Core: remove central core with seeds, used for apples, pears

Cream: mix together until blended, usually in reference to softened butter and sugar

Dash: less than 1/8 teaspoon

Done: test a baked product to be certain it is completely cooked

    Bread: 1) bake until brown and shrinks from side of pan
                  2) tap loaf, it should sound hollow

    Cakes: 1) when lightly touched with a finger the top springs back
                  2) cake pulls in a bit from edge of pan
                  3) a wooden toothpick inserted near center has no cake adhering to it when withdrawn

Fry: cook in fat (butter, margarine, or oil)

Grate: rub a food (usually lemons, oranges or cheese) on a grater to shred.

Grease: rub a small amount of fat onto a cooking or baking surface to prevent sticking of foods

Knead: mix dough with your hands until it is smooth and springy. Put dough on surface with 2 to 4 tablespoons of flour and a little flour on your hands. Lift the far half of dough toward you and press it down on the near half with the heels of your hands. Turn dough 1/4 turn and repeat. Continue to knead until smooth, 5 to 10 minutes; the more the better.

Peel: cut off the outside covering (usually for fruits and vegetables)

Roast: cook in the oven (usually in reference to meats or poultry)

Saute: cook in a small amount of fat

Simmer: place liquid over moderate heat. Bubbles do not come to the surface; cook food in liquid that is simmering

Slice: cut in thin flat pieces (commonly used for fresh tomatoes)

Stir: mix gently with spoon or fork

Stir-Fry: stir and lift foods constantly while sauteing over high heat

Toss: lift food pieces gently and allow them to fall back until mixed

Shopping Wisely

As it is for almost anything, list making assures success and acts as a reminder.

- Keep a running list handy. Tape it on a cabinet, put it on the refrigerator, or place it in a drawer in the kitchen. As you run out of items, add them to your list, right away, so you don't forget!
- Check local newspapers for specials, then you know what's a good buy. Plan a menu and add these items to your list.
- Check your cookbook for special ingredients in a recipe you want to try. Put these on your list.
- Shop once a week or less, if possible; plan food needs for the entire week as this saves time and money.
- Remember, no one food provides all the nutrients you need; eat a variety of foods.

Measurement Equivalents

1 tablespoon = 3 teaspoons
2 tablespoons = 1 ounce
1/4 cup = 4 tablespoons = 2 ounces
1/3 cup = 5 tablespoons + 1 teaspoon
1/2 cup = 8 tablespoons = 4 ounces
1 cup = 16 tablespoons = 8 ounces
1 pint = 2 cups = 16 ounces
1 quart = 4 cups = 32 ounces
1 gallon = 4 quarts = 128 ounces
1 pound flour = approximately 4 cups
1 pound white sugar = 3-1/4 cups
1 pound brown sugar = 2-1/4 cups
1 pound liquid (water, milk, etc.) = 2 cups = 1 pint
1 clove garlic = 1/8 teaspoon garlic powder
1 medium onion = 1 teaspoon onion powder = 1/4 cup finely chopped onion = 1 tablespoon minced dry onion
1 cup beef or chicken stock = 1 bouillon cube + 1 cup water = 1-1/2 teaspoon instant
   beef or chicken granules + 1 cup water

Kitchen Hints and Food Safety

- Keep **hot** foods **hot** and **cold** foods **cold.** Bacteria thrive in lukewarm, room temperature food. They multiply rapidly and can cause food poisoning.
- Place all leftovers in the refrigerator when meal is over. Cover them tightly to preserve freshness
- Dairy products, meats and vegetables should be kept refrigerated until ready to use.
- Do not refreeze thawed foods; refrigerate and use as soon as possible.
- Keep bread in its original wrapping; if not used in 2 or 3 days, refrigerate or freeze to discourage spoilage. If mold appears, dispose of entire loaf.
- Check canned goods before using; do not use those that are bulging or leaking. The good old maxim still holds true . . . "If in doubt, throw it out."
- Wash your hands with soap and water before handling food. Do not handle food if you have infected wounds or cuts on your hands.
- When washing dishes by hand, use hot soapy water. Wash glasses first, then silver-ware, plates, cooking utensils and last, pots and pans. Rinse in hot water. Drip dry in a drainer; put away.
- Never pour grease down the drain. Pour excess grease into an empty can and allow it to solidify, then discard.
- Lift covers from steaming saucepans away from yourself to avoid steam burn.

- Do not wear long, floppy sleeves when working in the kitchen near a gas flame or electric element.
- Turn handles of pans away from edge of range to prevent knocking them over accidentally.
- To prevent transfer of germs from raw poultry or raw meat to cooked poultry or cooked meat:
    Wash the platter or container that was used for the raw product before reuse.
    Clean cutting boards with a bleach solution: 1 teaspoon chlorine bleach to a quart of water.
- If eggs are to be eaten raw in a recipe, be sure to use eggs with uncracked shells. Eggs with cracked or broken shells are O.K. to use if they are cooked, such as in baking, scrambling, hard-cooking, etc.
- Finally, if food smells peculiar, looks peculiar or feels peculiar, throw it out or return it to the grocer if it warrants a refund.
- FIRE: the best fire extinguisher in your kitchen is baking soda. In a pinch, salt can be substituted. Keep both of these handy and close to your stove. NEVER use water to put out a grease fire, particularly near an electrical appliance.

Beverages

Even if you've never cooked before, you can create yummy drinks with little cost and effort, and in minutes be sipping the results!

Your kitchen becomes your own soda fountain with such dairy delights as Double Chocolate Soda (page 26) and Orange Freeze (page 25) and the busy day ahead becomes easier to face after enjoying a tall glass of Instant Orange Breakfast Drink (page 24).

Special party drinks are a "must" when you entertain. We've included some never-fail favorites, such as Wine Swizzler (page 27), Almost Champagne (page 27), Hot Mulled Cider (page 28) and Mexican Coffee (page 29).

Don't overlook the many varieties of coffees, teas and cocoa mixes available on the grocery shelf. Use your imagination and before long you'll be whipping up your own enticing liquid concoctions!

Instant Orange Breakfast Drink

The mix for this drink is good to keep handy in a screw-top jar. Leslie, a college student, always keeps a container of ice water in her dormitory refrigerator for mixing this quick and healthful breakfast drink.

The Mix:
1 cup instant non-fat milk
1/2 cup Tang instant orange drink
1/4 cup sugar

The Drink:
1 egg
1/2 cup Mix
1 cup ice water **or** milk
1/2 teaspoon vanilla extract (optional)

1. **Prepare** mix: combine all mix ingredients in a screw-top jar. Store tightly sealed.
2. **Prepare** drink: beat egg in bowl. Add mix, water and vanilla. Beat to a froth.
3. **Pour** into glass, enjoy! Makes 1 large glass.

Something Different: Substitute 1 cup chilled pineapple juice for the water and 1/4 teaspoon coconut extract for the vanilla.

 **Equipment** screw-top jar, small mixing bowl, measuring cups and spoons, beater, glass

Orange Freeze

A thirst-quencher special for a hot summer afternoon.

1 can (12 ounces) chilled orange soda
1 large spoonful orange sherbet (about 1/2 cup)

1. **Pour** soda into mixing bowl. Add sherbet.
2. **Beat** until blended and frothy. Pour into chilled glass. Serve immediately. Makes one tall glassful.

Something Different: Mix and match various sodas and sherbets for combinations you especially like. Try lemon/lime soda with lemon sherbet **or** raspberry soda with raspberry sherbet. Makes one tall glassful.

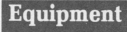 **Equipment** medium mixing bowl, mixing spoon, beater, 16-ounce glass

Good Old-Fashioned Ice Cream Sodas

From one of our daughters, Dana, who has worked in an ice cream parlor, comes this secret for making perfect ice cream sodas.

Double Chocolate
3 tablespoons chocolate syrup
1 cup chilled club soda
large spoonful chocolate ice cream (about 1/2 cup)
whipped cream and cherry (optional)

1. **Spoon** syrup, half of the soda and about 1 tablespoon of the ice cream into a chilled glass, stirring until smooth.
2. **Add** remainder of ice cream.
3. **Slowly Add** the rest of the soda until glass is full.
4. **Stir** gently and serve with a dollop of whipped cream and a cherry, if desired. Makes 1 serving.

Something Different: Very Vanilla: Omit chocolate syrup; substitute creme soda for club soda and vanilla ice cream for the chocolate ice cream. Simply Strawberry: In place of chocolate syrup use strawberry topping. Substitute strawberry ice cream for the chocolate ice cream.

 **Equipment** 16-ounce glass, measuring cup and spoons, spoon

Wine Swizzler

On a sizzler of a day try this swizzler of a drink!

1/2 cup wine (red, white or rosé)
1/2 cup chilled club soda
ice cubes
stemmed cherry

1. Pour wine and soda over ice cubes in a tall glass. Swizzle around with the stemmed cherry! Makes one serving.

Something Different: Almost Champagne: Combine equal amouts of chilled Sauterne wine and 7-Up in wine glasses.

Equipment tall glass, measuring cup

Hot Mulled Cider

This delicious cider and its companion, mulled wine, are perfect drinks to sip by the fire on a nippy evening. Take some in a thermos to a ball game or a special picnic.

1 quart apple cider **or** apple juice
1/4 cup firmly-packed brown sugar
1/4 teaspoon salt
1/2 teaspoon whole allspice
1 stick cinnamon
6 whole cloves
nutmeg (optional)

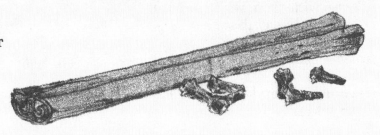

1. **Combine** all ingredients, except nutmeg, in saucepan. Bring to a boil.
2. **Reduce** heat to low and simmer, stirring occasionally, for 15 minutes.
3. **Serve** in mugs with a sprinkle of nutmeg for garnish. Makes 4 one-cup servings.

Something Different: Hot Mulled Wine: In place of apple cider, use 2 cups red wine and 2 cups water.

Equipment saucepan, measuring cups and spoons, mixing spoon

Mexican Coffee

Mexican coffee, traditionally rich and strong,is made with hot milk and cinnamon. Prepare just before serving. For a festive touch serve with a cinnamon stick in each cup.

2 tablespoons **each** instant coffee granules and sugar
1/2 teaspoon cinnamon
2 cups **each** milk and water

1. **Mix** coffee, sugar and cinnamon together in saucepan.
2. **Add** milk and water gradually, stirring until well mixed.
3. **Place** over medium heat. Stir occasionally until hot. **Do Not** boil.
4. **Serve** in coffee cups or mugs. A metal measuring cup can be used as a ladle. Makes 4 servings.

Equipment saucepan, measuring cups and spoons, mixing spoon

Snacks

When you're "simply starving" or when you're entertaining the gang, here are a variety of perfect snacks.

Some can be made ahead and stashed away for when you get the munchies. Tuck some in your lunch bag. And, don't overlook our hot treats that pop from the oven in minutes.

With today's fast pace of living, it's easy to overdo some snacks and neglect nutrition. In order to prevent that, keep plenty of fresh fruits and vegetables on hand for the quickest and healthiest snacks of all!

Chili Nuts

Hot and spicy. These store well for a week.

1/4 cup butter **or** margarine
4 cups whole walnuts, almonds **or** cashews
1 to 2 tablespoons chili powder (to taste)
1 teaspoon salt

1. **Melt** butter in a baking pan in 300°F. oven.
2. **Stir** in walnuts until coated with butter.
3. **Sprinkle** with chili powder and salt. Stir to mix.
4. **Return** to oven and bake for 20 minutes. Stir occasionally.
5. **Cool.** Stir occasionally.
6. **Store** in tightly covered container or plastic bag. Makes 4 cups.

Equipment

baking pan (8-inch square), measuring cups and spoons, mixing spoon

Popular Party Mix

Great to have on hand when you get a Munchie Attack—and it's not just junk food! This will keep well for days, so you can easily double the recipe.

1/4 cup margarine
2 teaspoons Worcestershire sauce
1 teaspoon garlic powder
1/2 teaspoon onion salt
1 cup **each** Wheat Chex, cheese-flavored croutons and Cheerios
1/2 cup **each** peanuts and small pretzels

1. **Melt** margarine with Worcestershire sauce, garlic powder and onion salt in 8-inch square baking pan in 275°F. oven.
2. **Stir** in remaining ingredients.
3. **Bake** for 30 minutes, stirring occasionally.
4. **Store** in tightly covered containers or in plastic bags. Makes 4 cups.

Something Different: Almost any cereal or nut combination can be used in this recipe. Try soybeans, sunflower seeds, pine nuts, Corn Chex, Bran Chex, or whatever . . . !

Equipment baking pan (8-inch square), measuring cups and spoons, mixing spoon

On the Trail Mix

We like this particular combination of ingredients, but you may substitute your own favorite nuts, seeds and dried fruits. The candy-coated chocolate is good on the trail because it doesn't melt.

1 cup any brand granola cereal
1 cup salted peanuts
1/2 cup raisins
1/2 cup coarsely chopped dried apricots, peaches, pears **or** pineapple
1 cup coated chocolate candies **or** carob chips

1. **Place** all ingredients in plastic bag and shake to mix.
2. **Store** in cool dry place in plastic bag secured with a wire twist. Makes 4 cups.

Equipment measuring cups, knife, plastic bag

Popcorn Jumbles

A terrific party snack that can be made ahead. Also good to crunch on while watching TV, writing a term paper or filing reports!

1/4 cup butter **or** margarine
1/2 cup firmly-packed brown sugar
2 tablespoons corn syrup
1/4 teaspoon salt

1/4 teaspoon baking soda
6 to 8 cups popped corn (popped
    according to package directions)
1 cup peanuts

1. **Melt** butter, sugar, syrup and salt in saucepan over medium heat. Bring to a boil, stirring constantly.
2. **Reduce** heat to low. Continue to boil mixture for five minutes, without stirring.
3. **Remove** from heat. Stir in baking soda.
4. **Combine** popcorn and peanuts on baking sheet. Pour syrup slowly over popcorn mixture. Stir to coat.
5. **Bake** at 250°F. for 1 hour, stirring every fifteen minutes.
6. **Cool** on baking sheet. Break apart and serve. Makes 9 to 10 cups.

Equipment saucepan, measuring cups and spoons, mixing spoon, baking sheet

Go-Go Granola Bars

These homemade granola bars make a nutritious and filling snack or a quick breakfast-on-the-go.

1/4 cup **each** margarine, firmly-packed brown sugar **and** peanut butter
2 tablespoons honey
2-1/4 cups any brand granola cereal
1/4 cup chopped walnuts **or** peanuts

1. **Melt** margarine, sugar, peanut butter and honey in saucepan over medium heat, stirring constantly.
2. **Remove** from heat and stir in granola and nuts.
3. **Press** into a well-greased 8-inch baking pan.
4. **Bake** at 350ºF. for 15 to 20 minutes, or until lightly browned.
5. **Cool** completely. Cut into bars. Makes 9 bars.

 **Equipment** saucepan, measuring cups and spoons, mixing spoon, baking pan (8-inch square), knife

All Occasion Dips

If you keep the basic dry mixes, sour cream and crackers on hand, you can whip up any of these dips when company drops in.

California Onion Dip
1 carton (2 cups) sour cream
1 envelope (1-1/2 ounces) dry onion soup mix

1. **Add** dry soup mix to sour cream. Blend with a fork.
2. **Serve** with chips, crackers or prepared raw vegetables. Makes 2 cups.

Something Different: Fiesta Dip: In place of onion soup mix, use 1 envelope taco seasoning mix. Serve with corn chips.
East India Dip: In place of onion soup mix, use one teaspoon curry powder. Serve with thin sesame crackers.
Dilly Dip: In place of onion soup mix, use one teaspoon dried dill weed and one teaspoon dried minced onion. Serve wtih raw vegetables, page 112.

Equipment small mixing bowl, fork

Four Star Cheese Spread

This zesty cheese spread can star four ways: as a sandwich filling, as a spread for celery sticks or crackers, as a dip and as a party cheese ball.

2 tablespoons butter or margarine
2 teaspoons Worcestershire sauce
1/2 teaspoon garlic powder
1 package (3 ounces) cream cheese, cut into chunks

1/4 cup crumbled Bleu cheese
1 cup grated Cheddar cheese
1 cup grated Monterey Jack cheese
parsley (optional)

1. **Melt** butter in saucepan over low heat. Remove from heat.
2. **Add** remaining ingredients in order given, mashing cheeses against sides of pan while blending.
3. **Place** in mixing bowl and refrigerate.
4. **Remove** from refrigerator an hour before serving for ease in spreading. Garnish with parsley, if desired. Serve with crackers. Makes about 2 cups.

Something Different: Festive Cheese "Apple": Form cheese mixture into a ball; garnish with a blush of paprika, and top with a sprig of mint or holly according to the season. Serve with crisp wedges of red apple.

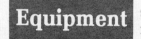 **Equipment** saucepan, medium mixing bowl, measuring cups and spoons, grater, mixing spoon

Guacamole

Carol loves to share this special recipe with friends. Her secret ingredients are finely chopped fresh onion and just the right amount of chili powder. To choose ripe avocados, look for ones with dark brownish green-colored skins. The flesh should "give" when squeezed.

2 ripe avocados, pitted and peeled
5 tablespoons finely chopped onion
1 tablespoon lemon juice
1 teaspoon salt
1/4 teaspoon chili powder
1/3 cup mayonnaise

1. **Mash** avocados with fork in mixing bowl. Stir in remaining ingredients and mix well.
2. **Refrigerate** covered until ready to use. Makes 1-1/2 cups.

 **Equipment** small mixing bowl, cutting board, knife, fork, measuring cups and spoons

Green Chile Quesadillas

Cindy, an active teen-ager, is never too busy to make, and eat, these hot snacks from South of the Border!

2 flour tortillas, 10-inch size
margarine
1/4 cup chopped green chiles
1/2 cup grated Monterey Jack cheese

1. **Spread** margarine on one side of each tortilla. Place spread side up on baking sheet.
2. **Divide** chiles and cheese into two equal portions and scatter on top of each tortilla.
3. **Bake** at 400°F. for 5 minutes, or until cheese is bubbly.
4. **Cut** in wedges and serve open-faced. Or, if you're really hungry, you may wish to fold each tortilla in half to eat as a sandwich! Makes 12 wedges or 2 sandwiches.

Something Different: In place of Monterey Jack, use a tangy Cheddar cheese.

Equipment baking sheet, measuring cups, knife, grater

Speedy Little Pizzas

When 12-year old Caryn tested this recipe for us, she said, "Hey! These are speedy little guys, aren't they?" So we decided to call them that. It's now a favorite of hers.

2 English muffins
1/2 cup prepared pizza sauce
8 pepperoni slices
4 thin slices of mozzarella cheese
oregano (optional)

1. **Split** muffins in half and place on baking sheet. Spread each half with 2 tablespoons pizza sauce.
2. **Top** each half with 2 slices pepperoni and 1 slice cheese. Sprinkle with oregano, if desired.
3. **Bake** at 400°F. for 10 minutes. Makes 4 little pizzas.

Something Different: Make your own specialty pizzas by adding your favorites; try chopped olives, sliced mushrooms, crumbled bacon, shrimp, anchovies or sausage.

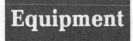 **Equipment** baking sheet, measuring cups and spoons, knife

Eggs

Eggs are a quick, easy and nutritious meal or snack. They are good any time of day. Because they are high in protein, eggs are an excellent meat substitute.

Store eggs or any food containing eggs in the refrigerator. Cook eggs slowly on medium heat so they are tender. High heat and fast cooking make eggs tough.

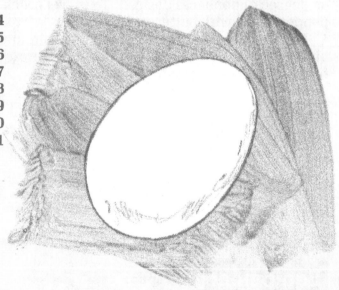

Soft and Hard-Cooked Eggs

1. Place eggs in single layer in saucepan. Add cold water to cover eggs plus one inch above. Cover with lid.

2. Bring water to brisk boil. Remove pan from heat.

3. For Soft-Cooked Eggs: let eggs remain in the hot water for 2 to 5 minutes, depending on degree of doneness desired. To serve: crack shell, spoon out egg, add butter, salt and pepper. Good with buttered toast.

4. For Hard-Cooked Eggs: let eggs remain in the hot water for 17 to 20 minutes. Drain and cover wtih cold water to cool. Refrigerate in shells. Use for deviled eggs, sandwich fillings, and potato salad.

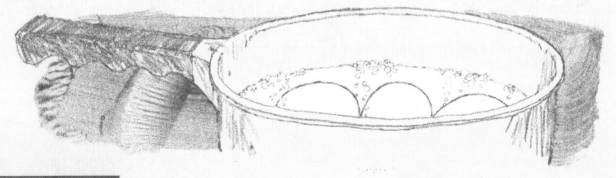

Equipment saucepan

Fried Egg

For a hot breakfast sandwich, place a fried egg and two slices of cooked bacon between two slices of buttered toast. Serve with fruit and a hot beverage.

1 tablespoon butter **or** margarine
1 egg

1. **Melt** butter in frying pan over medium heat.
2. **Break** egg carefully into pan so as not to break the yolk.
3. **Cook** until it is as firm as you like it.
4. **Turn** egg over with spatula **or** spoon the butter over the egg to glaze it or leave it "sunny side up." Makes 1 serving.

Something Different: Huevos Rancheros: When egg is almost done, spoon 1 to 3 tablespoons of prepared Salsa Sauce over egg and top with grated Monterey Jack or Cheddar cheese.

Equipment small frying pan, measuring spoon, spatula

Poached Egg

Serve on toast or toasted English muffin with fruit and a beverage.

1/2 teaspoon **each** salt and vinegar
1 egg

1. Add about two inches of water to saucepan with salt and vinegar. The vinegar makes the egg "set" faster. Bring the water to a simmer.
2. Break the egg over water and let it slide gently into the water without breaking the yolk.
3. Simmer 3 to 5 minutes until it is cooked the way you like it.
4. Lift the egg out of the water with slotted spoon. Makes 1 serving.

Something Different: Eggs Benedict: Place a thin slice of cooked ham on a toasted English muffin; top with poached egg and hot cheese sauce.

Equipment saucepan, measuring spoons, slotted spoon

Scrambled Egg

Add grated cheese, chopped green onions, sauteed mushrooms or cubed cooked ham to egg as it cooks. Serve with hash browned potatoes, toast and a beverage.

1 tablespoon butter **or** margarine
1 egg
1 tablespoon milk
dash **each** salt and pepper

1. **Melt** butter in frying pan over medium heat.
2. **Break** egg into bowl. Add milk, salt and pepper and beat with a fork.
3. **Pour** egg mixture into pan and stir (scramble) with a fork.
4. **Cook** to the consistency you like. Makes 1 serving.

Something Different: Scrambled Toast: Cut 1 slice of bread into cubes. Brown in margarine in frying pan. Add egg mixture and cook, stirring until desired consistency. Also good sprinkled with Parmesan cheese.

 **Equipment** small frying pan, bowl, measuring spoons, fork

Plain Omelet

2 eggs
2 tablespoons water
1/4 teaspoon salt

dash pepper
1 tablespoon butter or margarine

1. **Beat** eggs, water, salt and pepper together in bowl, using a fork, until blended.
2. **Melt** butter in frying pan over medium high heat until it sizzles. Lift and tilt pan to coat sides with butter.
3. **Pour** egg mixture into pan. Allow bottom layer of eggs to set slightly, about 10 to 20 seconds.
4. **Run** spatula around side of pan, lifting eggs, to allow the uncooked portion to flow underneath. Tilting pan helps. Continue this process until the top is barely set and still shiny. Total cooking time should be about one minute.
5. **Tilt** pan and gently fold omelet in half. If filling is used, spoon it on bottom half before folding.
6. **Tilt** again several times. Slide omelet out onto serving plate. Makes 1 serving.

Something Different: Spoon 1/4 to 1/2 cup cooked filling on bottom half before folding. You can use sauteed mushrooms, bits of cooked meat, chicken or seafood; creamed vegetables or your favorite cheese, grated.

 **Equipment** small bowl, fork, small frying pan, measuring spoons, spatula

48

Deviled Eggs

A good midday snack.

2 hard-cooked eggs (see page 49)
2 teaspoons mayonnaise
1/2 teaspoon pickle relish
dash **each** salt and pepper
dash paprika (optional)

1. **Remove** shells and slice eggs in half lengthwise. Lift out yolk with a teaspoon and place in mixing bowl.
2. **Mash** egg yolk with fork. Mix in mayonnaise, pickle relish, salt and pepper.
3. **Heap** egg yolk mixture back into center of egg whites.
4. **Sprinkle** with paprika. Chill and serve. Makes 2 servings.

Something Different: Add a dash of mustard, celery salt, chopped parsley **or** olives.

Equipment knife, teaspoon, small mixing bowl, fork, measuring spoons

49

Quiche

Oh so good! Even a "Getting Started" cook can put this together in a flash. For brunch, Lorna treats her friends to a variety of quiches, nutbreads, a fruit bowl and chilled white wine.

6 slices bacon, cut into small pieces
1/2 cup grated Swiss cheese
one 9-inch frozen deep-dish pie shell
3 eggs

3/4 cup half and half, light cream **or** milk
1/4 teaspoon salt
dash **each** nutmeg and pepper

1. **Fry** bacon in frying pan over medium heat until crisp. Drain well on paper towels and crumble.
2. **Sprinkle** bacon and cheese into pie shell.
3. **Beat** remaining ingredients together in mixing bowl. Pour into pie shell.
4. **Bake** at 375°F. for 30 to 35 minutes, or until knife inserted near center comes out clean.
5. **Let** stand 5 to 10 minutes before serving. Makes 4 servings.

Something Different: In place of bacon add 1/2 cup cooked cubed ham, meat, chicken **or** seafood.

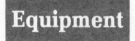 **Equipment** small frying pan, grater, small mixing bowl, measuring cups and spoons, beater

Brunch Souffle

When you entertain, assemble this casserole the previous evening and bake just before serving time. Serve it with Almost Champagne (page 27), Fruit Salad (page 104), Refrigerator Bran Muffins (page 146) and cups of steaming coffee.

5 slices pre-sliced French bread
1 pound bulk pork sausage
1 cup grated Cheddar cheese
3 eggs
1-1/2 cups milk

1/8 teaspoon salt
dash pepper
1/4 teaspoon prepared mustard
1 teaspoon Worcestershire sauce
1/2 can (10 ounces) cream of mushroom soup

1. **Cut** bread into 1-inch cubes.
2. **Cook** sausage in frying pan over medium heat and drain well.
3. **Place** bread cubes in greased 8-inch baking pan. Top with sausage and cheese.
4. **Combine** remaining ingredients in mixing bowl and beat well.
5. **Pour** egg mixture over ingredients in pan.
6. **Cover** and let stand in refrigerator overnight.
7. **Bake** uncovered at 350ºF. for 45 minutes. Cut into squares and serve. Makes about 4 servings.

 **Equipment** baking pan (8-inch square), cutting board, knife, large frying pan, mixing spoon, grater, large mixing bowl, measuring cups and spoons, beater, can opener

Sandwiches

We feature a wide choice of sandwiches made with a variety of breads, buns, crackers, sourdough rolls and pocket bread. You can make sandwiches that are open-faced, layered, grilled, dipped or fried. They are all easy and quick to make. For a light meal, serve a sandwich with fruit and a glass of milk. For a more hearty meal, serve your sandwich with soup, salad and a beverage.

When making sandwiches, use soft, room temperature butter or margarine so it doesn't tear the bread. Butter both slices of bread to the edges to keep the bread fresh and moist and to prevent the filling from soaking through. For variety, add sliced tomatoes, cucumbers, lettuce or watercress. Wrap the prepared sandwich to keep it fresh; use a plastic bag, plastic wrap or wax paper. Refrigerate until ready to serve.

Grilled Sandwiches

Grilled sandwiches are buttered on the outside and then grilled in a frying pan until they are toast crisp on each side and the cheese is melted. Choose your favorite fruit and beverage to go along with these tasty sandwiches.

Tuna Melt
2 slices bread
1/3 cup tuna filling (page 61)
1 slice American, Monterey Jack **or** Cheddar cheese
2 tablespoons butter **or** margarine

1. **Place** frying pan over medium heat.
2. **Assemble** sandwich; spread each slice of bread on one side only with butter.
3. **Place** one slice of bread, buttered side down, in frying pan. Top with filling and other slice of bread, buttered side up.
4. **Grill** sandwich 4 to 6 minutes on each side or until golden brown and cheese is melted. Makes 1 sandwich.

 **Equipment** small frying pan, measuring cups and spoons, knife, can opener, spatula

Grilled Cheese

2 slices bread
2 slices American cheese
2 tablespoons butter **or** margarine

1. **Follow** directions for Tuna Melt.

Pizza-wich

2 slices bread
3 tablespoons canned pizza sauce
4 slices salami
1 slice mozzarella cheese
2 tablespoons butter **or** margarine

1. **Follow** directions for Tuna Melt.

Patty Melt Sandwich

Here is another hearty sandwich. Use a cooked hamburger patty or slices of cooked meatloaf to make this all-American treat. Serve with crisp raw vegetables, a light dessert and your favorite beverage.

2 tablespoons mayonnaise
1 tablespoon chili sauce **or** catsup
1 tablespoon drained pickle relish
2 slices bread
1 cooked hamburger patty **or** several slices of cooked meatloaf
1 slice Cheddar **or** Swiss cheese
2 tablespoons chopped onion (optional)
1 tablespoon vegetable oil (optional)
2 tablespoons butter **or** margarine

1. **Gather** all ingredients. Place frying pan over medium-high heat.
2. **Mix** mayonnaise, chili sauce and pickle relish in mixing bowl. Spread evenly on one side of each slice of bread.

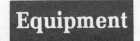 **Equipment** small frying pan, small mixing bowl, measuring spoons, spoon, knife, cutting board, spatula

3. Place meat and cheese on one slice (the side with relish spread) of bread.

4. Saute onions in oil in frying pan; spoon over meat.

5. Top with remaining slice of bread, relish side down. Butter outside of one slice of bread.

6. Place sandwich, buttered side down, in frying pan. Spread top of sandwich with butter.

7. Grill 4 to 6 minutes on each side, or until sandwich is golden brown and cheese is melted. Makes 1 sandwich.

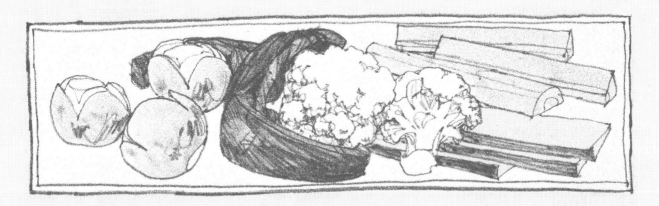

Reuben Sandwich

This robust grilled sandwich features Swiss cheese, corned beef and sauerkraut on rye bread. It is a meal in itself.

3 tablespoons mayonnaise
2 tablespoons chili sauce **or** catsup
2 tablespoons drained pickle relish
4 slices Russian rye bread

2 slices Swiss cheese
4 slices corned beef
1 can (8 ounces) sauerkraut, well-drained
2 tablespoons butter **or** margarine

1. Gather all ingredients. Place frying pan over medium heat.
2. Mix mayonnaise, chili sauce and pickle relish in mixing bowl. Spread evenly on one side of each slice xj
3. Arrange half the cheese, corned beef and sauerkraut on each of two slices of bread. Top with remaining slices of bread.
4. Spread top side of each sandwich with butter.
5. Place sandwiches, buttered side down, in frying pan. Spread tops of sandwiches with butter.
6. Grill sandwiches 4 to 6 minutes on each side or until sandwich is golden brown and cheese is melted. Makes 2 sandwiches.

 **Equipment** large frying pan, small mixing bowl, measuring spoons, spoon, knife, can opener, spatula

Monte Cristo Sandwich

A special continental treat for brunch, lunch or dinner. Serve with fruit salad and iced tea.

1 egg
2 tablespoons milk
1/4 teaspoon prepared mustard (optional)
1 tablespoon butter **or** margarine

2 slices bread
1 slice **each** cooked ham and
   turkey **or** chicken
1 slice Monterey Jack cheese

1. **Combine** egg, milk and mustard in 8-inch baking pan. Beat with fork until frothy.
2. **Assemble** sandwich by placing ham, turkey and cheese between slices of bread.
3. **Place** frying pan over medium-high heat. Add butter.
4. **Dip** sandwich into egg mixture, turning to coat both sides until all egg mixture has been absorbed.
5. **Place** sandwich in frying pan and fry until browned on each side and the cheese is melted. Makes 1 sandwich.

Something Different: Sprinkle with powdered sugar and serve with your favorite jam or jelly.

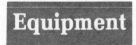 **Equipment** baking pan (8-inch square), measuring spoons, fork, small frying pan, spatula

Sandwich Filling

There is no limit to what you can stuff into pocket bread (also known as pita bread). The flat rounds when torn or cut in half, open to form pockets that are great for stuffing with one of our Sandwich Fillings (page 61) or your own.

A pocket sandwich is a "free-spirit" sandwich, so mix and match from each category as desired.

1. **Spread** the inside of pocket with a tablespoon or two of cream cheese, mayonnaise **or** butter.
2. **Stuff** with choice of tuna, chopped turkey, chicken **or** ham.
3. **Add** any one **or** two of the following: chopped lettuce, alfalfa sprouts, bean sprouts, sliced tomatoes, cucumbers **or** zucchini.
4. **Sprinkle** with chopped nuts, olives **or** bacon.
5. **Top** with your favorite salad dressing **or** taco sauce.

Equipment   knife

60

Pocket Bread Sandwiches

Tuna is our basic sandwich filling, but it is easy to vary as suggested in **Something Different** below. Use this sandwich filling on any type of bread, spoon it into pocket bread, stuff it into a hollowed out tomato for a lovely luncheon salad or serve on crackers as an hors d'oeuvres.

1 can (6-1/2 ounces) tuna, drained
1/4 cup finely chopped celery
1 tablespoon drained pickle relish
1 teaspoon prepared mustard (optional)
3 tablespoons mayonnaise **or** salad dressing
dash **each** salt and pepper

1. **Mix** all ingredients in bowl.
2. **Cover** and refrigerate until ready to use. Makes enough filling for 3 sandwiches.

Something Different: In place of tuna add 1 cup cooked chopped chicken, ham, salmon, crab, shrimp or hard cooked eggs.

 **Equipment** small mixing bowl, can opener, cutting board, knife, measuring spoons, fork

Steak Sandwich Au Jus

This is a fantastic sandwich for a Sunday night supper. For a perfect meal, serve with corn on the cob (page 121), wine and fresh fruit.

1 French roll, split in half
1 tablespoon mayonnaise
3 tomato slices
2 tablespoons butter **or** margarine
1/4 cup chopped onion
1/4 cup chopped green pepper
2 mushrooms, thinly sliced
1 thinly sliced breakfast **or** cube steak
1 teaspoon instant beef bouillon granules
1/2 cup warm water

1. **Spread** bottom half of the French roll with mayonnaise. Overlap tomato slices to fit on roll.
2. **Place** frying pan over medium-high heat. Melt butter in pan.

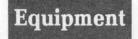 cutting board, knife, measuring cups and spoons, small frying pan, spatula

3. Saute onion, green pepper and mushrooms in frying pan. Remove vegetables and set aside.

4. Fry steak in same pan for two minutes on each side. Remove immediately to tomato-topped roll. Smother with cooked vegetable mixture.

5. Add bouillon and water to the drippings in the frying pan. Bring just to a boil, stirring to blend.

6. Dip top half of roll in the beef juice and place on sandwich. Enjoy!. Makes 1 sandwich.

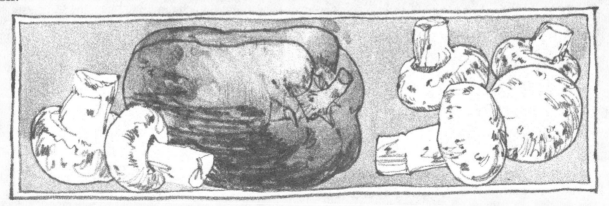

Soup

Soup can begin a meal, accompany a sandwich or serve as a hearty one-dish meal. The soups included in this chapter are easy and tasty. If you like, you can also buy canned soups or dried mixes from the market and dress them up with one of the following garnishes: chopped fresh parsley, green onions or chives, croutons, toasted nuts, crisp cooked bacon, crushed potato chips, bite-sized pretzels, crackers; sour cream or grated Parmesan cheese.

Simple Soup

This makes an elegant "first course" soup. The vegetables give it a oriental flavor.

1 can (10-3/4 ounces) condensed chicken broth
1 small peeled carrot, thinly sliced
1 small zuchinni, thinly sliced

1. Prepare broth according to instructions on can. Place over medium high heat in saucepan.
2. When soup comes to boil, add vegetables and simmer until they are just tender, about 3 minutes. Makes 2 servings.

Something Different: Substitute other thinly sliced vegetables, such as turnips, Chinese radishes or celery, for the carrot and zuchinni.

Equipment can opener, saucepan, vegetable peeler, knife, cutting board

Clam Chowder

If you like clam chowder, you'll make this recipe often. Vary the flavor by adding a can of creamed style corn or a can of tomatoes. Serve with hot buttered biscuits and apple pie (page 162).

3 slices bacon, cut into small pieces
1 medium onion, peeled and chopped
1 cup chopped celery
1/4 cup chopped green pepper (optional)
2 potatoes, peeled and cut into bite-sized pieces
2 cans (6-1/2 ounces each) minced clams, including juice
4 cups milk

1. **Place** Dutch oven over medium-high heat. Add bacon, onion, celery and green pepper.
2. **Saute** mixture in Dutch oven for 5 minutes.
3. **Add** potatoes, clams and milk. Simmer, **do not boil,** for 25 minutes. Serve steaming hot.
4. **Refrigerate** leftovers covered. Excellent reheated. Makes about 8 cups.

 **Equipment** Dutch oven, cutting board, knife, measuring cups, vegetable peeler, can opener, mixing spoon

Hearty Lentil Soup

For an economical and filling meal try this old-world favorite. Serve with crusty French bread, a glass of milk and fresh fruit for dessert.

2 cups water
1 cup dried lentils
2 cups tomato juice
1 can (10-1/2 ounces) beef broth
1 carrot, peeled and thinly sliced
1 cup thinly sliced celery

1 medium onion, peeled and chopped
1 cup thinly sliced cabbage
1 clove garlic, peeled and chopped
1/2 teaspoon salt
4 hot dogs, cut into bite-sized pieces **or**
    2 garlic sausages, sliced

1. **Bring** water to a boil over high heat in Dutch oven.
2. **Reduce** heat to low. Add lentils and simmer for 15 minutes.
3. **Add** remaining ingredients, except hot dogs. Cover and simmer for 35 minutes.
4. **Add** hot dogs and simmer 10 minutes longer. Serve steaming hot.
5. **Refrigerate** leftovers covered. Excellent reheated. Makes about 8 cups.

 **Equipment** Dutch oven, measuring cups and spoons, can opener, cutting board, knife, vegetable peeler, mixing spoon

Split Pea Soup

For a satisfying meal add a salad, a glass of milk and Campbell Cookies (page 175).

3 cups water
1 cup dried split peas
1 can (10-1/2 ounces) chicken broth **or**
   reconstituted bouillon
1 carrot, peeled and thinly sliced
1 cup chopped celery

1 medium onion, peeled and chopped
1 potato, peeled and cut in bite-sized pieces
1/8 teaspoon garlic powder
1/2 teaspoon salt
1 cup cut-up pieces of cooked ham

1. **Bring** water to boil over high heat in Dutch oven.
2. **Reduce** heat to low. Add peas and simmer for 30 to 40 minutes.
3. **Add** the remaining ingredients, except ham. Cover and simmer for 30 minutes.
4. **Add** ham and simmer 10 minutes longer. Serve steaming hot.
5. **Refrigerate** leftovers covered. Excellent reheated. Makes about 6 cups.

 **Equipment** Dutch oven, measuring cups and spoons, can opener, cutting board, knife, vegetable peeler, mixing spoon

Minestrone Soup

Everyone really likes this Minestrone soup and it goes together in minutes. For an even heartier meal, serve with a Grilled Cheese Sandwich and a glass of red wine or milk. Garnish steaming soup with Parmesan cheese.

3 strips bacon, cut into small pieces
1 clove garlic, peeled and chopped
1 cup chopped onion
1 carrot, peeled and sliced
1 rib celery, chopped
1/4 cup chopped parsley (optional)
1 can (16 ounces) cut green beans, including liquid
1 can (16 ounces) stewed tomatoes, including liquid
1 can (10-3/4) beef broth
1 can (8 ounces) kidney beans, drained
1/2 teaspoon salt
1/2 cup uncooked salad macaroni

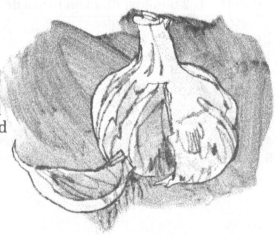

Equipment Dutch oven, cutting board, knife, measuring cups and spoons, can opener, mixing spoon

1. **Place** Dutch oven over medium-high heat.
2. **Saute** bacon, garlic and onions, stirring occasionally until bacon and onions are browned, about 7 minutes.
3. **Add** carrots, celery and parsley. Saute 5 minutes more, stirring occasionally.
4. **Add** green beans, tomatoes, beef broth, kidney beans and salt. Stir to mix.
5. **Reduce** heat to simmer. Cover pan and simmer 30 minutes, stirring occasionally.
6. **Add** macaroni. Continue simmering, covered, until macaroni is tender, about 10 minutes. Serve steaming hot.
7. **Refrigerate** leftovers covered. Excellent reheated. Makes about 8 cups.

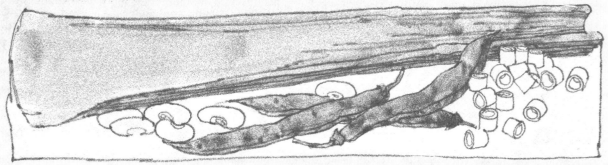

Main Dishes

Perhaps the best reason for getting started in the kitchen is to eat good main dish meals at home. They'll taste better and cost less than fast foods or frozen meals.

Look through this chapter for old stand-bys such as hamburgers, hot dogs and fried chicken. Try one of the simple casseroles or pan-meals. Discover how easy it is to cook a roast or steak. Creating a nutritious main course is not difficult, need not be time consuming and is definitely worth the effort.

Roast Beef

You won't believe how easy it is to roast beef. Ask your butcher to help you choose the right size and cut of beef.

Use an 8-inch baking pan for a small roast. For a large roast, line a baking sheet with aluminum foil, turning the edges up to make a rim to hold the juices. For 4 to 8 servings, use 2 to 4 pounds of beef. The following are appropriate cuts to use: standing rib roast, rolled rib roast, or sirloin tip roast. When ready to cook, place meat, fat side up in baking pan. Sprinkle with salt and pepper. **Do not** add water. **Do not** cover roast. Roast meat in a 325°F. oven. If meat is boneless, cook 25 to 35 minutes per pound for medium-rare. If meat has a bone, cook 22 to 26 minutes per pound for medium-rare. Add or subtract 5 minutes per pound for well done or rare. The most accurate way to check meat for doneness is to use a meat thermometer. For beef, 140°F. is rare, 150°F. is medium-rare and 160°F. is well done. Insert the thermometer into the thickest part of the meat. Be careful not to take the temperature next to the bone or in a fatty area. If you don't have a thermometer, check the roast by cutting a small, deep slit into the center of the roast. If the doneness is to your liking, remove the roast from the oven, if not, let it cook longer. Let the roast sit at room temperature for 10 minutes before slicing. This gives the juices a chance to retreat back into the roast, resulting in more succulent meat.

Equipment 8-inch baking pan, aluminum foil, meat thermometer

Pot Roast of Beef

This recipe allows for planned leftovers. After it has cooled, cover the roast with plastic wrap and store it in the refrigerator for up to one week. Thin slices of leftover roast make tasty sandwiches.

The chuck and brisket cuts of beef are usually more tender than the rump roast, so choose them first.

2 to 3 pounds beef chuck, brisket or rump roast
1 tablespoon vegetable oil
1 envelope (1-1/2 ounces) dry onion soup mix
1 cup beer, dry red wine **or** water

4 carrots, peeled and sliced
3 potatoes, peeled and cut into
  bite-sized cubes
4 stalks celery, sliced (optional)

1. **Place** Dutch oven over medium-high heat.
2. **Pour** oil into Dutch oven. After 30 seconds, add roast and brown well on all sides.
3. **Remove** Dutch oven from heat. Add soup mix and liquid.
4. **Cover** and bake in 300°F. oven for 2 to 2-1/2 hours.
5. **Add** carrots, potatoes and celery. Cook 1 hour longer, or until vegetables are cooked to desired doneness. Makes 4 servings.

 **Equipment** Dutch oven, measuring cup and spoons, vegetable peeler, knife, cutting board

Oriental Stir-Fry

Stir-fry dishes are quick all-in-one meals. If you want a larger meal, serve with cooked rice and a salad or fresh fruit. You may prefer to substitute asparagus, green beans, pea pods or zucchini for the broccoli.

2 teaspoons vegetable oil
1/4 pound beef, cut in thin bite-sized strips
1/4 cup thinly sliced onion
1 clove garlic, peeled and finely chopped
1 cup thinly sliced broccoli
1/2 cup fresh bean sprouts
1 tablespoon cornstarch
2 teaspoons brown sugar
1/4 teaspoon instant beef bouillon granules
3 tablespoons water
2 tablespoons wine **or** water
1 tablespoon soy sauce

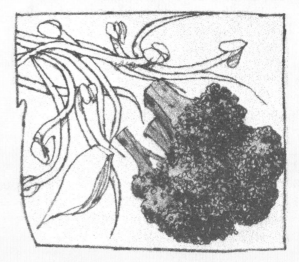

 cutting board, knife, measuring cups and spoons, large frying pan, slotted spoon

1. **Pour** oil in frying pan which has been placed over high heat.
2. **Add** meat, onion and garlic. Fry quickly, stirring constantly, until meat is browned.
3. **Lower** heat and stir in broccoli. Cover and simmer until tender, about 3 minutes.
4. **Add** bean sprouts.
5. **Combine** remaining ingredients in measuring cup and stir until cornstarch is dissolved.
6. **Pour** mixture over meat and cook stirring until thickened, about 3 minutes.
7. **Serve** immediately with additional soy sauce, if desired. Makes 1 generous serving.

Something Different: In place of beef, use chicken **or** ham.

Steak In a Pan

Our favorite pan-fried steak uses round or cube steak. To complete your meal serve with Fried Potatoes (page 120), and sliced tomatoes. Top it off with Chocolate Sticky Cake (page 168).

2 teaspoons butter **or** vegetable oil
1/4 to 1/2 pound top round steak **or** 1 cube steak
dash **each** garlic salt and onion salt
1/4 teaspoon **each** instant beef bouillon granules and prepared mustard
2 tablespoons red wine **or** water
1 teaspoon finely chopped fresh parsley

1. **Melt** butter in frying pan over medium-high heat.
2. **Fry** steak, turning to brown both sides (2 to 5 minutes per side depending on thickness of steak).
3. **Sprinkle** with salts.
4. **Remove** meat from pan. Add remaining ingredients to pan juices and cook over highest heat, stirring until very hot.
5. **Spoon** sauce over steak and serve. Makes 1 serving.

 **Equipment** small frying pan, measuring spoons, knife, spatula, spoon

Meat Loaf

Meatloaf is good plain or topped with your favorite barbeque sauce. Serve with Stir-Fry Broccoli (page 116) and a Chewy Butterscotch Bar (page 192).

1 pound lean ground beef
1/2 pound crushed Wheaties **or** bread crumbs
1/3 cup evaporated milk
1 teaspoon dried minced onion

1 teaspoon salt
dash pepper
2 potatoes, peeled (optional)

1. **Combine** all ingredients, except potatoes, in mixing bowl.
2. **Mix** together lightly, using your hands until thoroughly blended.
3. **Pat** meat mixture into shape of loaf. Place in baking pan.
4. **Arrange** potatoes in pan with meat loaf, if desired.
5. **Bake** in 350ºF. oven for 1 hour. Makes 2 servings.

Something Different: Meatballs: Shape mixture into 1 dozen meat balls. Brown in frying pan over medium heat. Place meatballs in 8-inch square pan. Pour 1 cup Sweet and Sour Sauce **or** Spaghetti Sauce over meatballs. Bake for 30 minutes at 350ºF. Serve over Steamed Rice (page 120) or cooked noodles.

Equipment medium mixing bowl, measuring cups and spoons, vegetable peeler, baking pan (8-inch square), can opener

Crunchy Tostadas

When David serves these at a party, he doubles the recipe and has each guest assemble his own tostada. The topping ingredients are served in mixing bowl, baking pans and his double boiler insert—anything clean and handy! David serves the meat mixture right out of the frying pan. His friends love his menu of Chili Nuts (page 32), iced tea, fresh fruit and Mexican Coffee (page 29).

1-1/4 pounds ground beef
1 can (16 ounces) refried beans
1/2 package (1-1/4 ounces) taco seasoning mix
1/3 cup water
1 package (10 ounces) corn chips
1-1/2 cups grated Cheddar cheese
3 to 4 cups chopped lettuce

2 tomatoes, chopped
1 small onion, thinly sliced
1 avocado, peeled and sliced
1 cup sour cream
1 can (3-1/4 ounces) pitted black olives
bottled taco sauce (any variety;
    hot or mild)

1. **Place** frying pan over medium high heat. Add beef. Saute until brown, breaking meat apart with spoon. Drain and discard fat when cooked.
2. **Stir** in beans, taco seasoning and water. Reduce heat to medium. Heat mixture thoroughly.

Equipment large frying pan, mixing spoon, can opener, cutting board, knife, grater, measuring cups

3. Assemble tostadas: place a handful of corn chips on an individual serving plate. Top with a large spoonful of meat mixture, then cheese, vegetables, sour cream, olives and taco sauce. Makes 4 servings.

Basic Ground Beef Mixture

You can prepare a delicious ground beef meal in minutes. You don't need pre-packaged "helpers" when you follow this basic recipe to make our Tacos, Burritos, Spaghetti and Meat Pie Favorite.

1 pound ground beef
1 small onion, peeled and chopped **or** 1 teaspoon dried minced onion
1 clove garlic, peeled and chopped **or** 1/8 teaspoon garlic powder
1/2 teaspoon salt
dash pepper

1. Saute all ingredients in frying pan over medium-high heat. Stir and crumble meat with a spoon and continue cooking until meat turns from pink to brown.
2. Push meat mixture to side of pan, tilt pan so that grease can be spooned out into an empty can. Let grease cool and solidify, then discard.
3. Use meat in one of the following recipes **or** refrigerate in a covered container and use as desired. Will keep up to 5 days.

 **Equipment** large frying pan, measuring spoons, cutting board, knife, mixing spoon

Tacos

Marty's favorite quick meal that's fun to make.

1 recipe Basic Ground Beef Mixture (page 82)
1/4 cup catsup **or** tomato sauce
1 teaspoon **each** chili powder and
　Worcestershire sauce
1/2 teaspoon dried leaf oregano, crushed
8 corn tortillas

1 cup grated Cheddar cheese
2 cups thinly sliced lettuce
1 small onion, chopped
2 tomatoes, sliced
bottled taco sauce (any variety;
　hot or mild)

1. Heat beef mixture, catsup, chili powder, Worcestershire sauce and oregano in frying pan over medium heat until hot and flavors are blended, about 10 minutes.
2. Prepare tortillas according to package instructions for making taco shells.
3. Fill each taco shell with a spoonful of hot beef mixture. Top with remaining ingredients. Makes 4 servings.

Something Different: Burritos: Add 1 can (8 ounces) refried beans to beef mixture. Use flour tortillas instead of corn tortillas and heat according to package instructions. Spoon about 1/2 cup of mixture in the center of each tortilla and fold like an envelope.

 **Equipment** large frying pan, can opener, measuring cups and spoons, mixing spoon, grater, cutting board, knife

Spaghetti

Serve with a tossed green salad, French bread and a glass of milk.

1 recipe Basic Ground Beef Mixture (page 82)
1 can (8 ounces) tomato sauce
1/2 teaspoon dried leaf oregano, crushed
1 can (4 ounces) mushroom pieces (optional)
6 ounces spaghetti **or** noodles (cooked according to package instruction)
1/2 cup grated Cheddar cheese **or** Parmesan cheese

1. Combine beef mixture, tomato sauce, oregano and mushrooms in frying pan on medium heat.
2. Simmer about 30 minutes.
3. Serve over cooked spaghetti or noodles. Sprinkle with cheese. Makes 4 servings.

Something Different: Sauce can be used as the sauce base for Speedy Little Pizzas (page 41).

Equipment large frying pan, Dutch oven, can opener, spoon, grater

Meat Pie Favorite

Serve with Creamy Cole Slaw (page 106) and Double Chocolate Soda (page 26).

1 recipe Basic Ground Beef Mixture (page 82)
1 can (10-1/2 ounces) condensed tomato soup
1 tablespoon Worcestershire sauce
2 cups instant mashed potatoes (prepared according to package instructions)
2 tablespoons chopped parsley

1. **Spoon** beef mixture into double boiler insert or small casserole dish.
2. **Mix** tomato soup and Worcestershire sauce in can and pour over beef mixture.
3. **Top** with potatoes. Sprinkle with parsley.
4. **Bake** at 350°F. for 20 minutes. Serve hot.
5. **Refrigerate** leftovers, covered. Excellent reheated. Makes 2 generous servings.

Equipment double boiler insert, can opener, measuring cups and spoons, sauce-pan, mixing spoon

85

Oven Chops

Eric prepares these pork chops with his special Colusa-grown rice and bakes them along with Apple Pie (page 162).

2 tablespoons margarine	dash garlic powder
1/2 cup white or brown rice	1-1/2 cups sliced carrots
2 to 4 pork or lamb chops	1 cup sliced onions
1/2 teaspoon salt	1 cup tomato sauce **or** V-8 juice
1/8 teaspoon pepper	1/2 cup water, dry white wine **or** beer

1. **Melt** margarine in frying pan in 350ºF. oven. Spread rice evenly over margarine.
2. **Cut** excess fat from chops. Arrange chops over rice. Sprinkle with salt, pepper and garlic powder.
3. **Layer** carrots and onions over meat.
4. **Pour** tomato sauce and water over all ingredients.
5. **Cover** pan with tight fitting lid or aluminum foil. Bake at 350ºF. for 1-1/2 hours, or until liquid is absorbed by rice and meat. Serve hot.
6. **Refrigerate** leftovers covered. Excellent reheated. Makes 2 generous servings.

Equipment large frying pan, measuring cups and spoons, knife

Stuffed Roast Cornish Game Hen

You don't have to feed a crowd to enjoy roast poultry! Cornish game hen is fun and easy to prepare and is inexpensive. Enjoy gourmet results without effort. Serve with Stewed Green Beans (page 125), Snacking Cake (page 167) and chilled white wine.

1 Cornish game hen, defrosted
2 tablespoons margarine
1/4 cup **each** chopped celery and chopped onion
2 cups dry bread cubes or croutons
1/2 teaspoon salt
1 teaspoon poultry seasoning
1/3 cup chicken broth **or** hot water
1 egg, lightly beaten

1. Rinse game hen under tap water and remove giblets.
2. Optional Step: Simmer neck and gizzard in 1 cup water for half an hour to make chicken broth for the dressing. If you choose not to do this, discard giblets.
3. Melt margarine in saucepan. Add celery and onions and saute for about 5 minutes. Remove from heat. Stir in remaining ingredients.

 **Equipment** saucepan, measuring cups and spoons, knife, cutting board, mixing spoon, pie pan (9-inch), wooden toothpicks, aluminum foil

4. Stuff neck and body cavities of game hen with bread mixture. Fold skin at neck back over stuffing and skewer through back with two wooden toothpicks to hold in place. Place a small square of foil over stuffing at opening of body cavity. Cover tips of drumsticks with foil to prevent drying out.

5. Place stuffed game hen in pie pan. Roast in oven at 400°F. for one hour. Makes 1 serving.

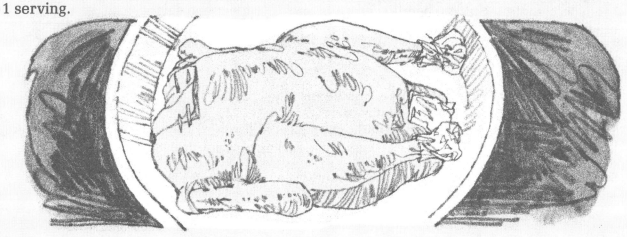

World's Easiest Chicken Dinner

Dave asked for a chicken recipe where everything is put in the pot and cooked in one step. We came up with this delicious chicken dinner for him.

1 fryer chicken, cut into serving-sized pieces
1/2 cup water
1 teaspoon instant chicken bouillon granules
1/2 cup dry white wine **or** chicken broth
3 medium potatoes, peeled and quartered
3 carrots, peeled and cut into 2-inch lengths

1 onion, sliced **or** 1 tablespoon
    dried minced onion
1 teaspoon salt
1/4 teaspoon pepper

1. **Rinse** chicken pieces under cool tap water.
2. **Place** chicken and remaining ingredients in Dutch oven. Cover with lid.
3. **Bring** to simmer on medium heat. Reduce heat to low and simmer for one hour, or until chicken is done. Makes 2 to 3 servings, depending on appetite!

Something Different: Add one or two of your favorite frozen vegetables the last 15 minutes of cooking.

 **Equipment** Dutch oven, measuring cups and spoons, knife, vegetable peeler, cutting board

No-Work Fried Chicken

Try this recipe for easy fried chicken. Then try one of our variations for "saucy" flavored chicken. Serve with a vegetable, Beer Biscuits (page 144), and a beverage.

2 tablespoons margarine
1/4 cup all-purpose flour
1 teaspoon salt
1/2 teaspoon pepper
2 **or** 3 chicken pieces

1. **Melt** margarine in 8-inch pan in oven.
2. **Measure** flour, salt and pepper into a clean paper sack.
3. **Shake** chicken pieces in the sack to coat evenly with the flour mixture.
4. **Remove** pan from oven. Roll chicken in melted margarine and leave in the pan, skin-side up.
5. **Bake** at 375ºF. for 45 minutes. Serve hot **or** cold. Makes 1 generous serving.

Something Different: Saucy Chicken: Instead of coating chicken pieces with flour mixture, spread 1/2 cup of barbeque sauce, sweet and sour sauce, spaghetti sauce, teriyaki sauce **or** jellied cranberry sauce evenly over the chicken. Bake at 350ºF. for 1 hour.

Equipment baking pan (8-inch square), paper sack, measuring cups and spoons

Souper Chicken and Rice

Serve with a glass of milk for a complete meal. If you prefer dark meat, use chicken legs instead of breasts.

1/2 cup rice
1 cup frozen carrots and peas
1 envelope Cream of Chicken Cup-A-Soup Mix
1 cup water
2 chicken breasts
1 envelope Onion Cup-A-Soup Mix

1. **Combine** rice, vegetables, cream of chicken soup mix and water in 8-inch baking pan.
2. **Top** with chicken.
3. **Sprinkle** with onion soup mix.
4. **Bake** at 375ºF. for 50 to 60 minutes or until chicken is browned and rice is tender. Makes 1 generous serving.

Something Different: In place of frozen carrots and peas, substitute frozen mixed vegetables.

Equipment baking pan (8-inch square), measuring cups, mixing spoon

Tater-Topped Franks

For a very quick supper between a day's work and an evening movie, serve these franks with sliced tomatoes and cucumbers.

2 frankfurters
2 servings instant mashed potatoes (prepared according to package instructions)
1 slice American cheese, cut in half
dash of onion salt

1. **Split** each frankfurter lengthwise, cutting almost, but not entirely, through. Spread them open, butterfly fashion, on pie pan.
2. **Spread** hot potatoes over frankfurters, dividing evenly.
3. **Place** half a slice of cheese on top of each tater-toped frank. Sprinkle with onion salt
4. **Bake** at 350ºF. for 15 minutes. Makes 1 generous serving.

 **Equipment** pie pan (9-inch), knife, saucepan, measuring cups and spoons

Spiced Beans and Hot Dogs

This is a meal in an instant for Steve when he comes home from a hard day's work famished. Serve with toasted English muffins, crunchy carrot sticks and milk.

1 can (31 ounces) Pork n' Beans
3 tablespoons **each** firmly-packed brown sugar and catsup
2 teaspoons dried minced onion
dash garlic salt **or** garlic powder
4 hot dogs

1. Mix all the ingredients, except hot dogs, together in sauce pan. Push the hot dogs down into the beans.
2. Cook over medium heat, stirring occasionally, until heated through. Makes 2 generous servings.

Equipment   saucepan, can opener, measuring spoons, mixing spoon

Crunchy Tuna Casserole

Bake this casserole right in the mixing bowl! Serve it with Refrigerator Bran Muffins (page 146), fresh, ripe melon and a beverage.

1 can (5 ounces) chow mein noodles
1 can (10 ounces) condensed Cream
   of Mushroom Soup
1/4 cup milk
1 cup thinly sliced celery

1 cup bean sprouts (optional)
1/4 cup sliced green onions, including tops
1 can (6-1/2 ounces) tuna, drained
1/2 cup cashew nuts

1. Reserve 1 cup chow mein noodles for topping. Pour remaining noodles into double boiler insert.
2. Mix remaining ingredients, except nuts, with noodles in mixing bowl. Top with nuts and reserved noodles.
3. Bake at 350ºF. for 40 minutes. Makes 4 servings.

Something Different: In place of tuna, use chopped cooked chicken **or** turkey.

 **Equipment**   double boiler insert, can opener, cutting board, knife, measuring cups

Saucy Fish Bake

Let your oven do the work while you sip a cool drink and watch the news! Easy Homebaked Bread (page 152) and One Pan Apple Torte (page 161) go nicely with this dish.

1 tablespoon butter **or** margarine
1/2 pound fish fillets (any white fish such as halibut, butterfish, sole, haddock or turbot)
1 tablespoon all-purpose flour
1/2 teaspoon salt
1/4 teaspoon pepper
1/4 teaspoon garlic powder (optional)
1/4 cup chopped onion
1 medium tomato, chopped
1 tablespoon **each** Worcestershire sauce and milk **or** cream

1. Heat oven to 375ºF. Melt butter in 8-inch baking pan in the oven. Remove pan from oven.
2. Sprinkle fillets on both sides with flour, salt, pepper and garlic powder.

 **Equipment** baking pan (8-inch square), knife, measuring cups and spoons, mixing spoon, fork

3. **Arrange** fillets in single layer in pan. Top with onion, tomato and Worcestershire sauce.

4. **Bake** at 375ºF. for 40 minutes or until fish flakes easily when prodded with a fork. Remove fish to serving plate.

5. **Add** milk to juices in pan, stirring until smooth and blended.

6. **Spoon** sauce over fish. Serve immediately. Makes 2 servings.

Salads

Although we may humorously call it "rabbit food," most of us have come to know and appreciate the flavor, freshness and color of a good salad. If you are concerned about all that chopping and peeling, don't fret. Our recipes make it easy to serve the individual appetite. Included are helpful hints that will give you plenty of "salad savvy," even when coping with larger salads for parties. And, you will see how easy it is to make your own zesty salad dressing.

Basic Tossed Green Salad

Use this recipe as an easy guide to make a salad for two. To serve a larger group, simply double, triple or even quadruple the quantity. To prepare greens for storage, wash thoroughly, shake off excess water and drain on paper towels. Store and chill greens in a plastic bag in the refrigerator. When ready to serve, tear or cut chilled greens into bite-sized pieces.

3 cups washed, chilled and torn or cut Greens (see page 101)
1 cup prepared Toss-Ins (try 3 or more varieties from page 101)
3 tablespoons Salad Dressing (pages 102 and 103)

1. **Pile** the Greens and Toss-Ins in mixing bowl.
2. **Toss** just before serving with Salad Dressing of your choice. Use mixing spoon for tossing.

Equipment large mixing bowl, knife, cutting board, measuring cups and spoons, mixing spoon

Greens:	**Vegetables:**	**Fruits:**	**Others:**
Butter lettuce	Beets, cooked	Apples	Cheese
Green leaf lettuce	Carrots	Avocadoes	Croutons
Red leaf lettuce	Celery	Grapefruit	Nuts
Romain	Cucumbers	Mandarin oranges	Olives
Spinach	Mushrooms	Oranges	Seeds (celery, sunflower)
Iceberg lettuce	Onions		Eggs, hard-cooked
Nappa cabbage	Green Peppers		Bacon pieces
(also called Chinese cabbage)	Radishes		
	Sprouts (alfalfa, bean)		
	Tomatoes		
	Zuchini		

Toss-Ins: wash well and peel if needed. Then thinly slice or cut into bite-sized chunks, if necessary.

Suggested combinations:

- **Greens:** spinach; **Toss-Ins:** onions, hard-cooked eggs, bacon pieces; **Dressing:** Bleu Cheese.
- **Greens:** Nappa cabbage; **Toss-Ins:** celery, onions, apples, sunflower seeds; **Dressing:** Italian.

Salad Dressings

Many good packaged salad dressing mixes are available. All you have to add is mayonnaise, buttermilk, oil, vinegar or water. There are also excellent ready-to-use bottled dressings. But, it's just as easy and lots cheaper to make your own dressing from a few basic ingredients. Here are a few good recipes.

Italian Dressing
2/3 cup vegetable oil
1/3 cup vinegar
1 clove garlic, peeled **or** 1/8 teaspoon garlic powder
2 tablespoons chopped onions **or** 1/2 teaspoon onion powder

1 teaspoon sugar
1/2 teaspoon salt
1/4 teaspoon pepper

1. **Combine** all ingredients in a two-cup, screw-top jar. Shake jar vigorously to mix ingredients.
2. **Store** covered in refrigerator. Shake dressing just before serving. Makes one cup.

Something Different: Add 2 tablespoons catsup, now it's French Dressing.

Equipment screw-top jar (2-cup), measuring cups and spoons, knife

Thousand Island Dressing

1 cup mayonnaise
1/2 cup catsup

2 tablespoons chopped pickle relish **or**
1/2 dill pickle, finely chopped

1. **Combine** all ingredients in a two-cup, screw-top jar. Stir with fork to mix.
2. **Store** covered in refrigerator. Makes 1-1/2 cups.

Blue Cheese Dressing

1 cup mayonnaise
1/4 cup sour cream
1 package (3 or 4 ounces) Blue cheese, crumbled
1/4 teaspoon **each** Worcestershire sauce and onion powder
1/8 teaspoon garlic powder

1. **Combine** all ingredients in a two-cup, screw-top jar. Mash and stir ingredients with a fork to mix.
2. **Stir** before using. Thin, if necessary, with one tablespoon milk. Makes 1-1/2 cups.
3. **Store** covered in refrigerator. Makes 1-1/2 cups.

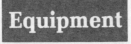 **Equipment** screw-top jar (2 cups), measuring cups and spoons, fork

Fruit Salad

These recipes use seasonal fresh fruit. Canned or frozen fruit may be substituted. For a quick fruit salad, use a combination of canned fruit or fruit cocktail.

Summer Fruit Salad
1 cup sliced peaches **or** apricots
1/2 cup sliced strawberries
1/2 cup seedless grapes
1 cup cubed cantaloupe
1 teaspoon honey
2 tablespoons orange juice

Winter Fruit Salad
1 cup chopped unpeeled red apple
1 cup cut-up orange sections
1 cup chopped unpeeled pears
1 teaspoon honey
2 tablespoons orange juice

1. **Combine** prepared fruit in mixing bowl.
2. **Stir** in honey and orange juice. Orange juice prevents fruit from darkening.
3. **Refrigerate** covered: Good the next day. Makes 2 generous servings.

 **Equipment** knife, cutting board, medium mixing bowl, measuring cups and spoons, mixing spoon

Sparkling Strawberry Squares

This luscious, tangy molded salad wakes up a ho-hum menu.

3/4 cup water
1 package (3 ounces) strawberry gelatin
1 can (8 ounces) crushed pineapple, with syrup
1 package (10 ounces) sliced frozen strawberries, partially thawed, with syrup
sour cream (optional)

1. Boil water in saucepan. Remove from heat. Add gelatin and stir until completely dissolved.
2. Stir in pineapple and strawberries.
3. Pour into 8-inch square baking pan and refrigerate until set, about 2 hours.
4. Cut into squares as needed. For a neat cut, run hot water over knife then cut with heated knife.
5. Serve with dollop of sour cream, if desired. Refrigerate extra salad covered. Makes 6 servings.

Something Different: Tangy Orange Squares: Substitute orange for strawberry gelatin and 1 can (8 ounces) mandarin oranges, wtih syrup, in place of strawberries.

Equipment saucepan, measuring cup, mixing spoon, can opener, baking pan (8-inch square)

Creamy Coleslaw

Make coleslaw using red, green or Nappa cabbage. It is very colorful if you use half red and half green.

2 cups thinly sliced or grated cabbage
2 tablespoons chopped green onion, including tops
1 rib celery, thinly sliced
1 tablespoon chopped green pepper
1 tablespoon **each** sugar and vinegar
1/4 teaspoon salt
1/2 cup crushed pineapple (optional)
1/2 cup mayonnaise
dash nutmeg (optional)

1. **Combine** all ingredients in mixing bowl. Toss lightly to mix.
2. **Refrigerate** covered. Good the next day. Makes 2 generous serving.

Something Different: Add 1/2 cup chopped unpeeled apple.

Equipment medium mixing bowl, knife, measuring cups and spoons, cutting board, mixing spoon

Potato or Macaroni Salad

This is a super make-ahead salad. Use either cooked potatoes or cooked macaroni. It is delicious either way. If you need salad for a large group, double or triple the recipe. Cook potatoes as directed on page 120 (3 to 4 medium potatoes equal about 3 cups). Cook macaroni according to package directions (1 cup raw macaroni cooks to about 3 cups).

3 cups diced, cooked potatoes **or** 3 cups cooked salad macaroni
3 hard-cooked eggs, chopped
2 ribs celery, chopped
1/2 cup chopped onion
2 tablespoons finely chopped parsley
1 tablespoon vinegar **or** dill pickle juice
1 teaspoon **each** salt and prepared mustard
1/8 teaspoon pepper
1 cup mayonnaise

1. **Combine** all ingredients in mixing bowl. Toss lightly to mix.
2. **Refrigerate** covered until ready to serve. Makes 2 generous servings.

 **Equipment** large mixing bowl, cutting board, knife, measuring cups and spoons, mixing spoon

Tuna Crunch Salad

Serve this elegant main dish salad with hot rolls and wedges of fresh pineapple.

1 cup cooked green beans, drained
1 can (6-1/2 ounces) tuna, drained
1/2 cup **each** chopped celery
  and water chestnuts
2 tablespoons **each** chopped green pepper
  and chopped green onions
1 tablespoon lemon juice

1/2 teaspoon salt
1/4 teaspoon onion powder
1/8 teaspoon garlic powder
1/2 cup mayonnaise
2 cups chow mein noodles
lettuce leaves

1. Combine all ingredients in mixing bowl, except noodles and lettuce leaves. Toss lightly to mix.

2. Refrigerate covered at least one hour or overnight, if desired.

3. Add noodles just before serving. Spoon mixture onto lettuce leaves. Makes 2 generous servings.

Something Different: Substitute cooked green peas for green beans and in place of tuna, use chopped, cooked chicken or turkey.

 **Equipment** large mixing bowl, measuring cups and spoons, cutting board, knife, can opener, mixing spoon

Taco Salad

1/2 pound ground beef
1/2 cup catsup **or** tomato juice
1/2 teaspoon **each** chili powder,
    cumin and salt
1/4 teaspoon **each** pepper and
    garlic powder
1 can (8 ounces) kidney beans, drained
1 cup crushed tortilla chips

1/4 head Iceberg lettuce, torn in
    bite-sized pieces
1 tomato, chopped
1 avocado, seeded, peeled, cut into chunks
2 green onions, including tops, thinly sliced
1 cup grated Cheddar cheese
1 can (4 ounces) chopped olives, drained
1/2 cup sour cream
1 can (4 ounces) chopped green chiles

1. **Saute** ground beef in frying pan, stirring, until meat turns brown. Drain and discard grease.
2. **Add** catsup, chili powder, cumin, salt, pepper, garlic powder and kidney beans. Stir to mix. Lower heat to simmer. Cover pan and cook 15 minutes.
3. **Combine** chips, lettuce, tomato, avocado, onions, cheese and olives in mixing bowl. Toss with mixing spoon.
4. **Pour** hot beef mixture over lettuce mixture just before serving. Toss quickly.
5. **Serve** garnished with sour cream and green chiles. Makes 2 generous servings.

Equipment small frying pan, measuring cups and spoons, large mixing bowl, knife, can opener, mixing spoon, cutting board

Vegetables

Vegetables are incredible. If you were to eat a different vegetable every day for 100 days, you would not have tasted all the existing vegetables. They are available fresh, frozen and canned. Most of them are good both raw and cooked. In this chapter you'll find some old favorites and some new ideas to tempt you.

Raw Garden Vegetables

Many vegetables you normally eat cooked are also delicious raw. Besides vegetables such as carrots, celery, green onions, green peppers and radishes, try a few different ones from the list below. Any of these vegetables are good served by themselves or with a Dunk In:

Asparagus: Wash well. Snap off and discard woody part of stem. Serve whole or sliced.
Broccoli: Wash well. Cut off coarse, woody part of stem. Cut off remaining tender stem and peel. Slice into pencil-like strips. Separate floweretts into bite-sized pieces.
Cauliflower: Wash well. Cut off leaves, then cut out part of core. Break or cut flowerets into bite-sized pieces.
Zucchini: Use the small tender size, about 6 inches long. Wash Well. Cut off stem and blossom end. Slice into long pieces.

Dunk Ins: Serve prepared vegetable with one of the following:
All Occassion Dips (page 37), yogurt, cottage cheese with nuts or chives, mayonnaise with lemon juice or curry, salad dressings (pages 102 and 103), peanut butter, taco sauce, guacamole (page 39), Four-Star Cheese Spread (page 38).

Equipment knife

Marinated Garden Vegetables

Toss freshly-cooked hot vegetables with oil, vinegar and blend of seasonings and marinate two hours or longer at room temperature. If you're too busy to mix up your own dressing, substitute prepared Italian-style dressing for the marinade.

Marinated Green Beans
1 pound fresh green beans
1 cup cleaned, sliced raw mushrooms
Marinade
1/3 cup vegetable oil
2 tablespoons vinegar
1 teaspoon prepared mustard
1/4 teaspoon salt
dash pepper
1/2 cup chopped green onions, including tops
1 tablespoon chopped parsley

1. Wash beans then snap off and discard stem end. Cook whole, in 1 inch of boiling salted water (1/2 teaspoon salt), until crisp tender, about 7 minutes. Cover pan during

Equipment saucepan, knife, measuring cups and spoons, cutting board, mixing spoon, screw-top jar

113

cooking. **Do not over cook.** Cooked beans should be bright green in color, not drab.

2. Shake together ingredients for marinade in a screw-top jar. Let stand.

3. Drain cooked beans well. Add raw mushrooms to cooked beans.

4. Pour marinade over hot beans and mushrooms. Toss to coat vegetables with marinade.

5. Marinate vegetables at room temperature for two hours or longer. Toss occasionally.

6. Serve at room temperature. Refrigerate leftovers covered. Excellent the next day. Makes 2 generous servings.

Something Different: Substitute one of the following vegetables for the green beans. Then follow recipe steps 2 through 6.

Fresh Carrots: Wash and peel 3 medium sized carrots. Cut into sticks or rounds. Cook until crisp tender.

Frozen Vegetables: Use one package (about 10 ounces) frozen broccoli, cauliflower, green beans **or** carrots. Cook as the package directs.

Canned Vegetables: Use one can (16 ounces) green beans, kidney beans, garbanzo beans, lima beans **or** carrots. Heat vegetable in saucepan.

Stir-Fried Garden Vegetables

Many vegetables are excellent stir-fried. Asparagus, Chinese snow peas, carrots, green beans, summer squash, broccoli, cauliflower and mushrooms are some of our favorites. Don't be afraid to make your own combinations.

Broccoli Stir-Fry

3/4 pound fresh broccoli (about 2 small stalks)
1 tablespoon vegetable oil, butter **or** margarine

1/2 teaspoon **each** salt and sugar
1/4 cup water

1. **Wash** broccoli. Cut off woody part of stem and trim blemishes off remaining stalk. Slice tender part of stalk in thin rounds. Break flowerets into bite-sized pieces. Set slices and flowerets aside.
2 **Heat** oil in frying pan. Add broccoli and saute over high heat, stirring constantly, for 2 minutes.
3. **Sprinkle** salt and sugar over broccoli. Add water and stir.
4 **Reduce** heat to simmer. Cover pan and cook about 8 minutes, stirring occasionally.
5. **Serve** hot, topped with butter or mayonnaise. Refrigerate leftovers covered. Good cold or reheated. Makes 2 generous servings.

 **Equipment** large frying pan, knife, cutting board, measuring cup and spoons, mixing spoon

Zucchini Stir-Fry

For a change of pace, substitute yellow crook-neck or patty pan squash for zucchini.

1/2 pound fresh zucchini
2 tablespoons **each** butter and chopped onion
1/2 teaspoon salt

1. **Wash** zucchini. Trim off ends. Slice in rounds or strips.
2. **Heat** butter in frying pan. Add zucchini, onion and salt. Saute over high heat, stirring constantly, about 2 minutes.
3. **Reduce** heat. Cover pan and simmer 5 minutes. Serve hot with pan juices. Refrigerate leftovers covered. Makes 2 generous servings.

Equipment large frying pan, knife, measuring spoons, cutting board, mixing spoon.

Mushroom Stir-Fry

Excellent served with steak or hamburgers.

1/4 pound fresh mushrooms
2 tablespoons butter
1 tablespoon vegetable oil

1. Wash mushrooms. Dry on paper towels. Trim off end of stem. Leave mushrooms whole or slice.
2. Heat butter and oil in frying pan. Add mushrooms. Saute on high heat, stirring, until lightly browned, about 5 minutes.
3. Serve with pan juices. Refrigerate leftovers covered. Excellent reheated. Makes 2 generous servings.

Equipment large frying pan, knife, measuring spoons, cutting board, mixing spoon.

Baked Fresh Vegetables

Many vegetables are delicious baked and it is a convenient way to cook them when the oven is being used for other components of the meal.

Baked Potatoes

Use Russet or Idaho potatoes for baking. Choose potatoes of uniform size (so they finish cooking at the same time). Store them in a cool, dark spot, until ready to use. Top baked potatoes with butter or sour cream and chopped chives.

Russet potatoes (one per person)   vegetable oil **or** margarine

1. **Scrub** potatoes well. Pierce in two places with a knife (holes allow steam to escape so potato won't explode in oven).
2. **Rub** potato skin with oil, using a paper towel or your hands.
3. **Bake** on oven rack at 325ºF. to 375ºF. Temperature can vary depending upon what else is being baked along with potatoes. A medium sized potato bakes in about 45 minutes. It is done when it gives a little when squeezed wtih your hands.

Something Different: Substitute sweet potatoes for the Russets.

 **Equipment** knife, mixing spoon, measuring spoon, baking sheet

118

Scalloped Potatoes

Scalloped potatoes are an all-time favorite, especially good served with ham. This recipe can be prepared, ready for the oven, in minutes. Serve with a small canned ham (bake following label), buttered green peas and a fruit salad or fruit dessert.

2 large potatoes, washed and peeled
1/2 clove garlic (optional)
1/2 cup **each** chopped onion and grated Cheddar cheese
2 tablespoons margarine

1/2 teaspoon salt
dash pepper
1/2 cup milk

1. **Slice** potatoes 1/8 inch thick. Rub inside of pie pan with cut side of garlic. Grease pan with a little of the margarine.
2. **Spread** half the potatoes in pan. Layer with half the onions, cheese, margarine, salt and pepper. Repeat.
3. **Pour** milk evenly over mixture. Bake uncovered, at 325°F. to 350°F. about 45 minutes, or until milk is absorbed and potatoes are tender. Top should be golden brown. Serve hot. Refrigerate leftovers covered. Excellent reheated. Makes 2 generous servings.

 **Equipment** pie pan (9-inch), knife, vegetable peeler, measuring cups and spoons, grater

119

Broccoli-Corn Casserole

This versatile dish goes beautifully with chicken, fish, ham, pork chops or roast beef. It is mildly-flavored but packed with nutrition.

1 egg
1 cup frozen chopped broccoli, thawed
1 can (8-3/4 ounces) cream-style corn
1 teaspoon dried minced onions
1/2 teaspoon salt
dash pepper
1/2 cup wheat cracker crumbs, divided
2 tablespoons butter **or** margarine, divided

1. **Beat** egg slightly in double boiler insert.
2. **Stir** in broccoli, corn, onion, salt and pepper and half each of the crumbs and butter.
3. **Combine** remaining crumbs and butter. Sprinkle over top of casserole.
4. **Bake** covered at 375°F. for 40 minutes or until bubbling hot. Makes 2 large servings.

 **Equipment** double boiler insert, measuring cups and spoons, fork

Baked Acorn Squash

1 medium acorn squash (also called Danish squash)
2 tablespoons butter
2 tablespoons brown sugar
salt and pepper

1. **Cut** (no easy matter) squash in half, from stem to bottom. Scoop away seeds with sturdy spoon.
2. **Place** cut-side down on baking sheet. Bake near middle of oven at 350ºF., about 45 minutes.
3. **Remove** baking sheet from oven. Turn squash cut-side up. Mash the pulp slightly, in the shell, with the edge of spoon.
4. **Season** each half with butter, brown sugar, salt and pepper
5. **Return** squash to oven for about 10 minutes, until butter is melted and squash is tender. Refrigerate leftovers covered. Good reheated. Makes 2 servings.

Something Different: Substitute a small butternut squash or a one-pound piece of banana squash.

Equipment knife, mixing spoon, measuring spoon, baking sheet

Boiled Fresh Vegetables

Boiled New Potatoes

New potatoes, both red and white skinned varieties, are found in the cooled produce section of the market. Buy potatoes of uniform size (so they finish cooking at the same time) and refrigerate until ready to use. Both varieties are excellent to use for scalloped potatoes and potato salad because they hold together and don't fall apart or break easily when cooked and sliced.

potatoes
cold water and salt

1. **Scrub** potatoes. Place whole unpeeled potatoes in saucepan. Add water to cover and 1 teaspoon salt.
2. **Bring** water to boil. Lower heat, cover pan and boil gently about 30 minutes. Potatoes are cooked when they pierce easily with a fork.
3. **Serve** hot in skins or peeled. Cut open and top with butter, salt and pepper. Refrigerate leftovers.

Equipment saucepan or Dutch oven

Corn on the Cob

Fresh corn is available from early summer through the fall. It is sweetest when cooked immediately after picking, which explains why locally grown corn is so delicious.

Fresh corn on the cob (one ear or more per person)
boiling, unsalted water

1. **Half Fill** Dutch oven with hot water. Bring to full boil over high heat.
2. **Husk** corn. Break off stem end and remove all silk. Rinse well.
3. **Plunge** ears carefully into boiling water. Cover pot and cook at full boil 5 minutes.
4. **Remove** from heat and drain off water. Keep corn in pan, covered, until ready to serve.
5. **Serve** hot with butter, salt and pepper.

Something Different: Cut kernels off cob of cooked corn with sharp knife and saute in 2 tablespoons butter. Salt and pepper lightly, **or** follow Corn Skillet recipe (page 124), substituting fresh corn kernels for canned.

 **Equipment** Dutch oven

Frozen Vegetables

There are dozens of excellent frozen vegetables available in various package sizes. Some are packaged in large plastic bags which are handy because you pour out what you need, close the bag with a wire twist and return it to the freezer for future use. Cooking and serving directions are on all packages. Always use the least amount of water and the shortest cooking time possible. For a change, try these recipes:

Green Peas Saute

2 slices bacon, cut in small pieces
2 tablespoons chopped onion

2 tablespoons sliced almonds (optional)
1 package (about 10 ounces) frozen green peas

1. Saute bacon, onions and almonds in saucepan until golden brown, about 5 minutes. Stir mixture as it cooks.
2. Add peas and stir to mix. Lower heat, cover pan and cook 5 minutes, stirring occasionally.
3. Serve hot with pan juices. Makes 2 generous servings.

Something Different: Green Bean Saute: Use green beans instead of peas. Cook beans 8 minutes, in step 2.

 **Equipment** saucepan, knife, cutting board, measuring spoons, mixing spoon

Creamed Spinach

This is a handy recipe which can be cooked in a saucepan on top of the stove or baked in a greased loaf pan. Try baking it along with No-Work Fried Chicken (page 91) and Beer Bread (page 144).

1 package (about 10 ounces) chopped frozen spinach, thawed and drained
2 tablespoons dried onion soup mix
1/2 cup sour cream **or** yogurt
nutmeg

1. **Stir** spinach, soup mix and sour cream together in saucepan.
2. **Cook** over low heat, stirring occasionally, until spinach is hot, about 5 minutes.
3. **Sprinkle** nutmeg over cooked spinach and serve immediately. Makes 2 generous servings.

Something Different: Baked Creamed Spinach: Follow above recipe through Step 1. Spoon mixture into a small greased loaf pan and sprinkle with nutmeg. Bake at 325°F. until hot and bubbly, about 20 minutes.

 **Equipment** saucepan, fork, measuring cup and spoons

125

Canned Vegetables

Canned vegetables are cooked and ready to eat. Most of them taste good hot or cold. The following recipes make canned vegetables taste even better.

Asparagus or Beets

1 can (8 ounces) asparagus **or** beets, drained (chill juice for a refreshing beverage)
1/4 cup mayonnaise, yogurt **or** sour cream
1/4 teaspoon tarragon **or** dill weed

1. Arrange vegetables on individual salad plates or a platter.
2 Top vegetables with mayonnaise and sprinkle with tarragon. Makes 2 generous servings.

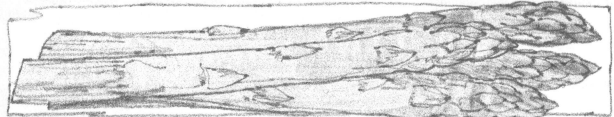

Equipment can opener, measuring cup and spoons, large frying pan, mixing spoon, saucepan, knife.

Stewed Tomatoes or Green Beans

1 can (16 ounces) whole tomatoes **or** cut green beans
2 tablespoons **each** chopped fresh parsley and chopped green onions
1 tablespoon butter **or** margarine
1/2 teaspoon basil **or** dried leaf oregano (optional)
dash salt and pepper

1. **Place** all ingredients in saucepan and stir to mix.
2. **Cover** pan and simmer 15 minutes, stirring occasionally. Makes 2 generous servings.

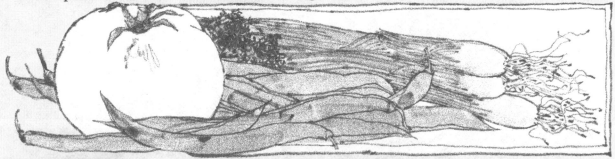

Equipment can opener, measuring cup and spoons, large frying pan, mixing spoon, saucepan, knife.

127

Rice and Pasta

Rice is available in a variety of forms: regular and quick cooking; long, medium and short grain; brown and white. All are good and having such a wide choice is what makes rice a popular menu item. Flavor variations are easy—simply vary the cooking liquid. Chicken broth and beef bouillon are two tasty alternatives. Interesting textures are achieved by tossing other ingredients such as nuts, mushrooms or fruits into the cooked rice. Learning to cook rice properly is an accomplishment to be proud of. We hope our step-by-step recipe will help you produce perfect rice every time.

Pastas include spaghetti, macaroni and egg noodles in a myriad of shapes ranging from bow-ties to wheels and twisties. Package instructions give the cooking time for each type. All pasta tastes better cooked "al dente," which means barely tender. Pasta should never be served mushy. Always cook it just before you are ready to serve it.

Pasta is delicious mixed with almost anything—sauces, cooked meat, seafood or poultry, cheeses and vegetables. It's also good plain, topped with butter, salt and pepper. The following recipes are quick, easy and great tasting.

Steamed Rice

This recipe may be doubled if you need extra servings or want to have rice leftover for making fried rice later.

1/2 cup regular long grain white **or** brown rice
1 cup water, beef **or** chicken broth
1 tablespoon margarine
1/2 teaspoon salt

1. Add all ingredients to saucepan. Bring mixture to a boil. Stir to mix. Lower heat to simmer.
2. Cover with a tight fitting lid or with aluminum foil. Cook 15 minutes for white rice or 45 to 50 minutes for brown rice. Test for doneness but do not stir. If rice is not tender or if liquid is not absorbed, replace lid and cook 5 minutes longer. Serve hot. Refrigerate leftovers covered. Makes about 1-1/2 cups.

Something Different: Add one or all of these ingredients in Step 1: 2 tablespoons chopped onions, parsley, celery, green pepper **or** mushrooms.

Equipment saucepan, measuring cups and spoons, mixing spoon

Fried Rice

Use cooked rice in this recipe. If you wish, add cooked meat to the rice (see **Something Different**) for a filling meal. Pass the soy sauce.

2 tablespoons vegetable oil **or** margarine
1/4 cup chopped green onions, including tops
2 tablespoons chopped celery
2 tablespoons chopped green pepper (optional)
2 cups cold cooked rice
1 egg

1. Heat oil in frying pan. Add onions, celery and green pepper. Saute over medium heat, stirring constantly, for 5 minutes.
2. Add rice and egg. Stir to mix and continue cooking until mixture is hot, about 5 minutes.
3. Serve immediately. Refrigerate leftovers covered. Makes 2 generous servings.

Something Different: Add one of the following ingredients to Step 1: 1/2 cup cooked ham, pork, beef, chicken **or** seafood.

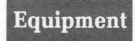 **Equipment** large frying pan, measuring cups and spoons, knife, mixing spoon, cutting board

Fettuccini "Getting Started"

This can be ready in about 15 minutes, start to finish. Serve with a tossed green salad and hot buttered French bread.

4 cups (6 ounces) Fettuccini egg noodles
2 tablespoons butter **or** margarine
1/3 cup cream **or** milk
1 cup firmly packed grated Swiss **or** Parmesan cheese

1 **Cook** noodles in saucepan according to package directions, until barely tender.
2. **Drain** off water immediately and completely. In same pan, stir in remaining ingredients.
3. **Cook** over medium-high heat, stirring until cheese is melted and mixture is hot, about 4 minutes.
4. **Serve** immediately. Refrigerate leftovers covered. They are tasty the next day cold or reheated. Makes 2 generous servings.

Something Different: Mix in 2 tablespoons chopped green onions or parsley **or** add 1 can (4 ounces) chopped mushrooms, **or** next time, use green noodles.

 **Equipment** saucepan, mixing spoon, measuring cups and spoons, grater

Macaroni and Cheese

A good old standby that can be prepared on short notice. Serve it with hot buttered green beans and a glass of milk.

1-1/2 cups salad macaroni
1 tablespoon margarine
1 cup grated Cheddar **or** American cheese
1/2 cup milk

1 teaspoon prepared mustard
1/4 teaspoon salt
1/8 teaspoon pepper

1. **Cook** macaroni in saucepan according to package directions, until barely tender.
2. **Drain** off water. In same saucepan, stir in remaining ingredients.
3. **Cook** over medium heat, stirring until cheese is melted and mixture is hot, about 4 minutes.
4. **Serve** immediately. Refrigerate leftovers covered. Good the next day, cold or reheated. Makes 2 generous servings.

Something Different: Add 1 can (6-1/2 ounces) tuna, chunky ham or chunky chicken in Step 2 and follow recipe above.

Equipment saucepan, measuring cups and spoons, grater, mixing spoon

Noodles Romanoff

Make this dish ahead and bake just before serving. Bake Brownies (page 171) with the noodles and to complete the meal add Marinated Garden Vegetables (page 114).

3 cups (8 ounces) twistie egg noodles
1/2 cup **each** cottage cheese, yogurt and milk
3 tablespoons chopped onion
1/2 teaspoon Worcestershire sauce
1/4 teaspoon salt
1/8 teaspoon **each** pepper and garlic powder
1/2 cup grated Swiss **or** mozzarella cheese

1. **Cook** noodles in a saucepan according to package directions, until barely tender.
2. **Drain** off water. In same saucepan, mix in remaining ingredients, except Swiss cheese.
3. **Pour** mixture into greased baking pan. Top with Swiss cheese.
4. **Bake** at 325°F. for 30 minutes, uncovered.
5. **Serve** hot. Refrigerate leftovers covered. Good reheated. Makes 2 generous servings.

 **Equipment** saucepan, measuring cups and spoons, knife, grater, mixing spoon, baking pan (8-inch square)

Spaghetti Casserole

This casserole can be made ahead, refrigerated and reheated.

1-1/4 pounds ground beef
1/3 cup chopped onion
1 clove garlic, peeled and finely chopped
3 cups (6 ounces) Spaghetti Rings **or** flat noodles
1 teaspoon dried leaf oregano, crushed

1/2 teaspoon salt
1/2 can (10-3/4 ounces) tomato soup
1-1/2 cups water
1 cup grated Cheddar cheese

1. **Saute** beef, onion, and garlic in frying pan until browned, breaking it up with mixing spoon. Drain.
2. **Place** uncooked spaghetti rings in baking pan. Top with meat mixture. Sprinkle with oregano and salt.
3. **Spoon** soup over meat mixture. Pour water over all.
4. **Cover** with foil and bake at 350°F. for 1 hour.
5. **Sprinkle** with cheese. Return to oven and bake uncovered for 15 minutes.
6. **If** making ahead, refrigerate at this point. To reheat, cover with foil and bake at 350°F. for 40 to 45 minutes or until bubbly. Makes about 4 servings.

Equipment large frying pan, cutting board, knife, mixing spoon, measuring cups and spoons, baking pan (8-inch square), aluminum foil

Breads

For centuries breads have been a basic part of our diets, but it's the homebaked variety, with its fetching aroma, that gives a special lift to the simplest meal.

Grocery stores and bakeries provide many good breads, as well as a variety of good mixes, but we think you will find it just as convenient and more economical to bake your own breads following our recipes. Once you've started, you'll discover the experience is exciting, almost magical. The results will delight everybody.

Zucchini Nut Bread

Zucchini Nut Bread is a favorite. You'll love this recipe because it's so versatile. When you tire of zucchini, use this recipe to make pineapple, carrot, banana or pumpkin bread too. Nut bread is delicious toasted for breakfast or great served with a salad for a light lunch and these little loaves make perfect gifts. Make them ahead when you have time, wrap tightly in plastic wrap or aluminum foil and freeze until the gift-giving occasion.

2 eggs
1/2 cup vegetable oil
3/4 cup sugar
1 teaspoon vanilla
1/4 cup plain yogurt
1-1/2 cups all-purpose flour
1/2 teaspoon **each** salt, baking soda and baking powder
1 teaspoon cinnamon
1 cup grated raw unpeeled zucchini
1/2 cup chopped walnuts

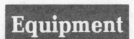

Equipment 2 loaf pans (5 x 3 x 2 inches), large mixing bowl, measuring cups and spoons, mixing spoon, knife, grater, rubber scraper

1. **Mix** eggs, oil, sugar, vanilla and yogurt in mixing bowl with a spoon. Stir in flour, salt, baking soda, baking powder and cinnamon. Beat well.

2. **Add** zucchini and nuts. Stir, mixing thoroughly.

3. **Pour** equal amounts of batter into well-greased loaf pans, using scraper to clean bowl of all batter.

4. **Bake** at 375°F. for 45 minutes, or until bread tests done.

5. **Cool** in pan for 10 minutes before removing. Makes 2 small loaves.

Something Different: In place of zucchini use **one** of the following variations: 1 can (8 ounces) well drained, crushed pineapple, and 1/2 cup flaky coconut, **or** 1 cup grated carrots and 1/2 cup raisins, **or** 3/4 cup mashed ripe banana, **or** 3/4 cup mashed pumpkin and 1/2 cup miniature chocolate chips.

Orange Brunch Cake

An easy-to-prepare morning treat with the brisk and refreshing tang of orange.

1-1/2 cups all-purpose flour
2 teaspoons baking powder
1/2 teaspoon baking soda
1/2 cup sugar
1 tablespoon grated orange peel
1/3 cup **each** orange juice and plain yogurt
1 egg
1/4 cup vegetable oil

Topping:
1/4 cup sugar
1 teaspoon cinnamon

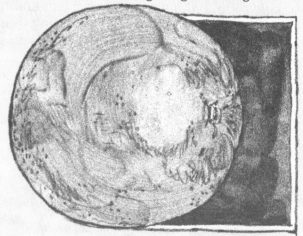

1. Stir flour, baking powder, soda and sugar together with a fork in large mixing bowl.
2. Grate one side of orange for the peel. Cut orange in half and squeeze the grated half for the juice. Cut the other half orange in slices to serve with the cake.

Equipment large mixing bowl, small mixing bowl, measuring cups and spoons, fork, grater, rubber scraper, baking pan (8-inch square)

140

3. **Mix** orange peel, juice, yogurt, egg and oil in small mixing bowl.
4. **Pour** orange mixture into flour mixture. Stir quickly with a fork to blend.
5. **Pour** batter into greased baking pan, using rubber scraper to clean bowl.
6. **Combine** topping ingredients and sprinkle over batter.
7. **Bake** at 400°F. for 25 minutes, or until cake tests done.
8. **Cut** in squares. Best served hot from the oven. Makes 9 squares.

Brenda's Butterhorns

Our version of a county fair Blue Ribbon winner. They taste like cheese Danish and are best served warm. For a change of pace, serve with your favorite jam or jelly.

Rolls:
1/4 cup butter **or** margarine, room temperature
1/2 cup cottage cheese
1/2 cup all-purpose flour

Topping:
1/4 cup powdered sugar
1/4 teaspoon vanilla
2-1/2 teaspoons milk

1. Mix butter and cottage cheese in bowl. Stir until well blended.
2. Stir in flour, mixing until dough sticks together. Cover with plastic wrap or waxed paper and refrigerate overnight.
3. Place chilled dough on lightly floured (about 1/4 cup) cutting board or waxed paper. Pat into 10-inch circle.

 **Equipment** medium mixing bowl, measuring cups and spoons, mixing spoon, cutting board, knife, baking sheet

4. Cut into 4 or 8 wedges, depending upon size of rolls desired. Roll each wedge, beginning at the rounded edge, toward point. Repeat for each wedge.

5. Place rolls on greased baking sheet. Bake at 350°F. for 30 minutes or until lightly browned.

6. Combine the topping ingredients in a measuring cup. Mix until smooth.

7. Spread topping over warm rolls. Makes 4 large or 8 small rolls.

Beer Biscuits

Quick as a wink you can create delicious crusty, tender biscuits or muffins with this unusual recipe. The extra beer can be refrigerated and used for this recipe again later. Even if it turns flat, it will work fine.

1 cup packaged biscuit mix
1 tablespoon sugar
1/3 cup beer

1. **Stir** all the ingredients together in mixing bowl.
2. **Drop** on well-greased baking sheet two inches apart or fill well-greased muffin pans 2/3 full.
3. **Bake** at 375°F. for 20 minutes, or until lightly browned. Let set for 2 minutes before removing from pan. Makes 6 biscuits or muffins.

Something Different: Beer Bread: Place dough in well-greased loaf pan (5 x 3 x 2 inches). Bake 30 minutes, or until top is golden brown and bread tests done.

 **Equipment** small mixing bowl, measuring cups and spoons, mixing spoon, baking sheet or muffin pan

Gladie's Pull Apart Rolls

This is our speedy version of a zesty, spicy dinner roll.

1 tablespoon butter
1/2 teaspoon dried minced onion
1/2 teaspoon dill seed
1 can (10 biscuits) refrigerated baking powder biscuits

1. **Melt** butter in small frying pan. Stir in seasonings.
2. **Dip** each unbaked biscuit in butter mixture. Stand biscuits on end, close together in loaf pan.
3. **Bake** at 375°F. for 20 to 25 minutes, or until lightly browned. Remove "loaf" from pan and serve warm. Makes 1 loaf

Equipment small frying pan, measuring spoons, spoon, loaf pan (5 x 3 x 2 inch)

Refrigerator Bran Muffins

Batter may be refrigerated in a covered container, such as a quart jar, for up to 2 weeks. Freshly baked muffins are just minutes away! Gently spoon batter into muffin cups. Pop them into the oven and while they bake you can get ready for work.

3/4 cup sugar
1/4 cup vegetable oil
1 egg
1-1/2 cups buttermilk

1-1/2 cups All-Bran **or** Bran Buds cereal
1-1/4 cups whole wheat flour **or** all-purpose flour
1/4 teaspoon salt
1-1/4 teaspoons baking soda

1. **Stir** sugar, oil and egg together in mixing bowl. Add buttermilk and cereal. Stir well to mix.
2. **Mix** in flour, salt and baking soda. Batter may be stored in refrigerator at this point.
3. **Spoon** batter gently into well-greased muffin cups. Bake at 375ºF. for 20 minutes. Refrigerate extra batter in covered container. Makes 12 muffins.

Something Different: Add 1/2 cup chopped dried fruit, such as raisins or dates and 1/4 cup chopped walnuts.

 **Equipment** large mixing bowl, measuring cups and spoons, mixing spoon, muffin pan, covered quart container

Pancakes

Pancakes are a favorite at any meal. Top with syrup, applesauce or, for a special treat, stack them and top with fresh sliced strawberries and whipped cream. To avoid mealtime rush make this batter when you have a free minute, then refrigerate it. Batter will keep one week. Spoon out and cook only what you need.

1-1/4 cups milk
1 egg
2 tablespoons sugar
1/2 teaspoon salt

2-1/2 teaspoons baking powder
1-1/4 cups all-purpose flour
1 tablespoon vegetable oil

1. Put all ingredients, except vegetable oil, in a jar or mixing bowl and stir with fork until smooth.
2. Heat frying pan on medium heat. To test frying pan for heat sprinkle a few drops of water on it. If bubbles dance on the surface, heat is right. Add oil.
3. Drop spoonfuls of batter in frying pan. Turn pancakes when top is bubbly and underside is nicely browned. Turn only once. Makes six 4-inch pancakes.

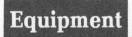 **Equipment** screw-top pint jar or medium mixing bowl, measuring cups and spoons, fork, mixing spoon, large frying pan, spatula

Oven Pancake

Enjoy this as a hearty meal for breakfast, lunch or dinner. Using few ingredients, it can be ready in a wink. The pancake puffs up like a popover. It is good topped with syrup, sprinkled with powdered sugar or spread with jam. The pancake goes well with ham, bacon or sausage and your favorite fruit.

1/4 cup butter **or** margarine
4 eggs
1 tablespoon sugar (optional)

1/8 teaspoon nutmeg (optional)
1 cup all-purpose flour
1 cup milk

1. **Melt** butter in frying pan in 400°F. oven.
2. **Beat** eggs, sugar and nutmeg vigorously in mixing bowl with a fork. Add flour and milk, stirring until mixed, but not smooth.
3. **Pour** batter into melted butter in hot frying pan. Bake at 400°F. for 15 to 20 minutes, until edges and top are golden brown.
4. **Cut** into wedges and serve immediately. The puffiness goes down rapidly, but it's supposed to. Makes 2 generous servings.

Equipment large frying pan (oven-proof), large mixing bowl, measuring cups and spoons, fork

French Toast

Use your favorite bread to make French Toast. It's best if the bread is at least a day or two old. Serve French Toast hot with Favorite Pancake Syrup (page 151) or spread tart jam or jelly on top.

1 tablespoon butter **or** margarine
1 egg
1/4 cup milk
dash of salt
1 teaspoon sugar (optional)
2 **or** 3 slices bread

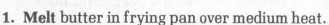

1. **Melt** butter in frying pan over medium heat.
2. **Beat** egg in pie pan with a fork. Add milk, salt and sugar. Mix well.
3. **Soak** both sides of bread in egg mixture.
4. **Place** bread slices in frying pan and fry until golden brown, about 4 minutes on each side. Makes one serving.

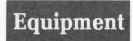

Equipment   **pie pan (9-inch), large frying pan, fork, measuring cup and spoons, spatula**

Favorite Pancake syrup

We prefer this handy homemade syrup to the commercial variety. It's thick, rich and buttery in flavor.

1 cup firmly-packed brown sugar
1/2 cup water
2 tablespoons butter
1 teaspoon vanilla (optional)

1. **Add** sugar, water and butter to saucepan. Bring to a rolling boil, stirring to mix.
2. **Remove** from heat. Stir in vanilla.
3. **Refrigerate** extra syrup in screw-top jar. Reheat by placing uncovered jar in pan of hot water. If syrup is too thick, add 2 to 4 tablespoons water. Makes one cup.

Something Different: Add 1/2 teaspoon cinnamon.

 **Equipment** saucepan, measuring cups and spoons, mixing spoon

Easy Homebaked Bread

Our easiest bread recipe: this takes only two hours from start to finish. The dough can be baked in two small loaf pans or it can be shaped into one large round loaf and baked on a cookie sheet. The same dough makes great cinnamon rolls.

1 package (1/4 ounce) active dry yeast
2 tablespoons sugar
2 teaspoons salt
1/4 cup vegetable oil
1 cup very warm water
2-1/2 to 3-1/2 cups all-purpose flour

1. **Mix** all ingredients, except flour, in mixing bowl. Stir well with spoon.
2. **Heat** oven to warm. While oven is warming, grease pans. Turn oven off.
3. **Add** flour gradually to yeast mixture, stirring vigorously, until dough forms a ball.
4. **Place** dough on lightly floured (about 1/4 cup) baking sheet or cutting board. Dust hands with flour and knead dough about 2 minutes. If you want to make cinnamon rolls see **Something Different** on next page.

Equipment

Easy Homebaked Bread: large mixing bowl, measuring cups and spoons, mixing spoon, 2 loaf pans (5 x 3 x 2 inches), baking sheet (or cutting board). Cinnamon Rolls: baking pan (8-inch square), measuring cups and spoons, knife

5. **Divide** dough in half. Shape into loaves and place in greased pans.

6. **Set** pans of dough in warmed oven and let rise until doubled in bulk, about 1 hour.

7. **Turn** on oven to 350°F. and bake 25 to 30 minutes or until top is golden brown and bread tests done.

8. **Remove** bread from pans and let cool. Store cooled bread in plastic bag secured with wire twist. Makes 2 small loaves.

Something Different: Cinnamon Rolls "A La Brian." Use bread recipe through Step 4, then do this:

1. **On** floured baking sheet, pat and press dough with hands to edge of baking sheet.

2. **Spread** 1/4 cup softened margarine over the dough. Sprinkle with 1/4 cup **each** brown sugar and white sugar and 1 tablespoon cinnamon. Roll up tightly, beginning at side. Seal by pinching edge of dough into roll. Cut into 20 one-inch slices. Place side by side, cut side down, in well greased 8-inch baking pan.

3. **Set** pan of rolls in warmed oven. Let rise until doubled in bulk.

4. **Turn** on oven to 350°F. and bake 20 to 30 minutes or until tops are golden brown.

5. **Immediately** invert pan on heat-proof serving plate, leaving rolls gooey side up. Makes 20 cinnamon rolls.

Three Wheat Batter Bread

For an interesting shape, try baking this bread in a well-greased one pound coffee can. It works perfectly.

1 package (1/4 ounce) active dry yeast
1/4 cup warm water
1/8 teaspoon ginger
2 teaspoons honey
2/3 cup (small can) evaporated milk
1 tablespoon water
2 tablespoons vegetable oil
1/2 teaspoon salt
1-1/4 cups all-purpose flour
3/4 cup whole wheat flour
1/4 cup wheat germ
2 tablespoons cracked wheat

1. Combine yeast, water, ginger and honey in a mixing bowl. Let stand until foamy, about 20 minutes.

large mixing bowl, measuring cups and spoons, can opener, mixing spoon, 2 loaf pans (5 x 3 x 2 inches) or a one pound coffee can.

2. **Stir** milk, water, oil and salt into yeast mixture, mixing well with spoon. Stir in flours, wheat germ and cracked wheat. Mix thoroughly.
3. **Divide** batter equally between two greased loaf pans. Cover with plastic wrap or waxed paper.
4. **Let** rise in a warm place until doubled in bulk, about 1-1/2 hours.
5. **Remove** cover. Bake at 350°F. about 30 to 40 minutes or until nicely browned.
6. **Remove** from pans and cool before slicing. Makes 2 small loaves.

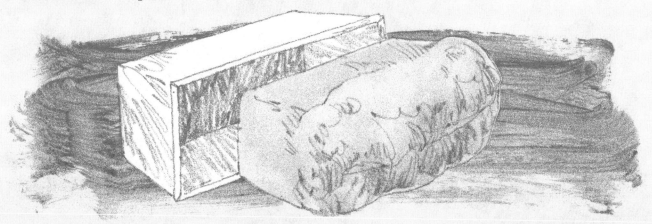

Desserts

People's eating habits have changed in the last few years. The trend is toward less filling meals that contain fewer calories. Desserts, because they are often calorie-laden, heavy and rich, are often skipped. This is unfortunate, because a well-chosen dessert tops off a meal in a most satisfying way. Choose a dessert to complement the meal: a hearty entree needs a light dessert, such as our Fruit Ice (page 160). A light entree, such as fish, may be followed by a more substantial dessert, such as Mocha Freezer Pie (page164).

Fresh Fruit in Cream

We particularly like strawberries in this recipe but grapes, sliced peaches or melon cubes are also delicious served this way.

2 cups small strawberries **or** large berries cut in half
1/3 cup sour cream
2 tablespoons brown sugar

Topping:
2 tablespoons **each** sour cream and brown sugar

1. **Wash** strawberries and remove stems.
2. **Combine** and gently mix fruit, sour cream and brown sugar in mixing bowl.
3. **Spoon** into serving bowls.
4. **Top** with sour cream and sprinkle with brown sugar. Makes 2 servings.

Something Different: In place of sour cream and sugar, spoon prepared vanilla pudding (6 ounce can) over the fruit.

 **Equipment** medium mixing bowl, knife, measuring cups and spoons, mixing spoon, 2 serving bowls

158

Pink Lady Yogurt

As pretty as it is simple.

1 cup water
1 package (3 ounces) raspberry gelatin
1 carton (8 ounces) red raspberry yogurt

1. Bring water to boil in saucepan. Remove from heat. Add gelatin and stir until dissolved.
2. Stir in yogurt until blended. Pour into 8-inch square pan.
3. Refrigerate at least three hours. Cut into squares using a table knife heated under hot tap water. Makes 6 servings.

Something Different: Substitute your favorite flavors. Try mixed fruit gelatin with peach yogurt; lime gelatin wtih lemon yogurt; strawberry-banana gelatin with banana yogurt. There's no end to wonderful combinations.

Equipment saucepan, baking pan (8-inch square), mixing spoon, measuring cups, knife

Fruit Ice

A cool dessert for summer, a refreshing dessert after a hearty winter meal.

1-1/2 teaspoons (1/2 package) unflavored gelatin
1/4 cup cold water
1/2 cup **each** sugar and water
1 can (5-1/2 ounces) grape juice
1/4 cup orange juice
2 tablespoons lemon juice

1. **Stir** gelatin into 1/4 cup cold water. Set aside to soften.
2. **Mix** sugar and 1/2 cup water in saucepan. Boil until sugar dissolves. Remove from heat.
3. **Add** gelatin mixture and remaining ingredients to sugar mixture. Mix well.
4. **Pour** into loaf pan and freeze. To serve, break up with fork and serve in small bowls. Makes 2 servings.

Something Different: In place of grape and orange juice, use a 12-ounce can of fruit nectar and 1 teaspoon lemon juice. Strawberry nectar makes a fantastic ice.

 **Equipment** saucepan, loaf pan (5 x 3 x 2 inches), measuring cups and spoons, mixing spoon, fork

One Pan Apple Torte

This is Carey Jean's idea of a great recipe . . . measure everything right into the pan, stir and bake!

1/4 cup vegetable oil
1 egg
3/4 cup white **or** firmly-packed brown sugar, **or** a combination of both
2 teaspoons lemon juice
1 teaspoon **each** cinnamon and baking soda
4 apples, peeled, cored and cut into 1/2-inch pieces
1 cup all-purpose flour
1 cup chopped walnuts **or** 1/2 cup chopped walnuts and 1/2 cup raisins

1. **Combine** oil, egg, sugar, lemon juice, cinnamon and baking soda in the baking pan. Stir with fork. Add apples. Stir to mix.
2. **Sprinkle** flour and nuts over mixture. Stir only until just mixed.
3. **Bake** at 350ºF. for about 35 minutes. Makes about 6 servings.

Something Different: In place of apples use fresh peaches or pears.

 **Equipment** baking pan (8-inch square), measuring cups and spoons, vegetable peeler, knife, fork

Apple Pie

The crumbly topping makes this pie even better. Use a pie crust shell from the frozen food section of the supermarket. They are unbaked and ready for your favorite fruit, pudding, or quiche filling.

4 apples, peeled, cored, cut in 1/4-inch slices
1/3 cup sugar
1 tablespoon flour
1/2 teaspoon cinnamon
1/4 teaspoon nutmeg
2 tablespoons lemon juice
one 9-inch pie crust shell, unbaked

Crumb Topping
1/3 cup **each** flour and sugar
3 tablespoons margarine

1. **Mix** apples, sugar, flour, spices and lemon juice in mixing bowl. Pile into pie crust.
2. **Mix** crumb topping ingredients in same bowl until well blended. Sprinkle over apples.
3. **Bake** at 375ºF. about 45 minutes or until apples are tender when tested with a fork.
4. **Serve** hot with ice cream or a slice of Cheddar cheese. Makes 6 servings.

 **Equipment** large mixing bowl, vegetable peeler, knife, measuring cups and spoons, mixing spoon

Grasshopper Pie

A perfect company dessert because it's pretty, delicious and is made several hours before serving.

16 chocolate sandwich cookies
1/4 cup butter **or** margarine
2/3 cup milk
24 large marshmallows

2 cups Cool-Whip **or** 1 cup whipping cream, whipped
1/4 cup green creme de menthe
2 tablespoons white creme de cocoa

1. **Crush** cookies in plastic bag with a jar used as a rolling pin.
2. **Melt** butter in saucepan.
3. **Combine** crumbs and butter in pie pan. Mix well. Reserve 1/2 cup mixture for topping. Press remainder onto bottom and sides of pie pan. Chill.
4. **Heat** milk and marshmallows in saucepan. Stir until marshmallows are melted. Cool in refrigerator for 30 minutes.
5. **Add** remaining ingredients. Mix well.
6. **Pour** into crust. Sprinkle with reserved crumbs.
7. **Cover** and freeze at least 4 hours. Makes 6 to 8 servings.

 **Equipment** saucepan, pie pan (9-inch), measuring cups and spoons, mixing spoon, jar or rolling pin, plastic bag

Mocha Freezer Pie

This pie requires a bit of planning due to the various steps of freezing. Liane finds the planning definitely worthwhile. We agree!

3 tablespoons margarine
14 chocolate sandwich cookies
2 squares unsweetened chocolate
1/2 cup sugar
1 tablespoon margarine
2/3 cup (1 small can) evaporated milk
1 pint (2 cups) coffee ice cream
1 cup Cool-Whip **or** 1/2 cup whipping cream, whipped
2 tablespoons Kahlua liquor (optional)
1/4 cup chopped nuts

1. Melt 3 tablespoons margarine in double boiler insert over direct heat.
2. Crush cookies in plastic bag with a jar used as a rolling pin. Put crumbs in pie pan and add melted margarine. Mix well and press firmly onto bottom and sides of pan. Place in freezer.

 **Equipment** plastic bag, jar or rolling pin, pie pan (9-inch), measuring cups and spoons, double boiler, mixing spoon, knife, can opener

3. **Melt** chocolate, sugar and 1 tablespoon margarine in double boiler insert over simmering water. Slowly pour in milk. Cook until thickened, stirring constantly. Refrigerate to cool.

4. **Remove** ice cream from freezer and let soften (up to 15 minutes). Fill pie shell with ice cream.

5. **Spread** cooled chocolate mixture over ice cream and return to freezer.

6. **Mix** Cool-Whip and Kahlua in measuring cup. Spread over pie and sprinkle with nuts. Return to freezer until serving time. Makes 8 servings.

Snacking Cake

This cake really appeals to Jim who hates to do dishes. It's mixed in the baking pan so there's hardly any mess. The only trick is to mix the ingredients thoroughly.

1-1/2 cups all-purpose flour
1 teaspoon **each** baking soda and cinnamon
1/2 teaspoon **each** cloves, nutmeg, allspice and salt
1 cup sugar
6 tablespoons vegetable oil
1 tablespoon vinegar
1 teaspoon vanilla
1 cup water
1/2 cup chopped walnuts (optional)

1. **Combine** flour, baking soda, spices, salt and sugar in baking pan. Stir until well mixed.
2. **Add** remaining ingredients. Mix thoroughly.
3. **Bake** at 350ºF. for 35 to 45 minutes or until cake tests done. Makes 6 to 8 servings.

 **Equipment** measuring cups and spoons, baking pan (8-inch square), mixing spoon

Chocolate Sticky Cake

Chandy's favorite! A rich, sticky, chewy chocolate cake.

Cake
1/2 cup **each** water and butter **or** margarine
2 tablespoons cocoa
1 cup **each** all-purpose flour and sugar
1 teaspoon baking soda
1 egg
1/4 cup milk
1/2 teaspoon **each** vanilla and salt

Frosting
1/4 cup butter **or** margarine
2 tablespoons cocoa
3 tablespoons milk
2 cups powdered sugar
1/2 teaspoon vanilla
1/2 cup chopped walnuts (optional)

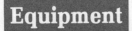 **Equipment** saucepan, measuring cups and spoons, mixing spoon, rubber scraper, baking pan (8-inch square)

168

1. **Heat** water, butter and cocoa in saucepan until butter is melted. Stir to blend. Remove from heat.
2. **Stir** in flour, sugar and baking soda.
3. **Beat** in egg, milk, vanilla and salt.
4. **Pour** into well-greased baking pan using rubber scraper.
5. **Bake** at 350ºF. for 35 minutes **or** until cake tests done.
6. **Heat** butter, cocoa and milk for frosting in same saucepan. Stir to blend and remove from heat.
7. **Mix** in powdered sugar and vanilla. Stir until smooth.
8. **Pour** frosting over warm cake. Sprinkle with nuts.
9. **Cool** thoroughly before cutting. Makes 12 servings.

Fruit Puddin' Cake

This is an ideal "oven-meal" dessert. Bake it in the oven along with the main dish and vegetables and you have a dessert without any extra oven time.

1 can (1 pound, 6 ounces) cherry pie filling
1 package (9 ounces) yellow **or** white Jiffy Cake Mix
1/2 cup **each** margarine and chopped walnuts **or** pecans

1. **Pour** pie filling into baking pan. Sprinkle dry cake mix over top of filling.
2. **Melt** margarine in saucepan. Pour over cake mix and sprinkle with nuts.
3. **Bake** at 350°F. for 45 minutes or until cake tests done. Serve warm or cool. Makes 6 servings.

Something Different: In place of cherry use blueberry, apple or peach pie filling.

Equipment baking pan (8-inch square), measuring cups, saucepan, rubber scraper

Brownies

Brownies are one of the all-time favorites of chocolate lovers like Anne. For a heavenly dessert, top with ice cream and hot fudge sauce

2 squares (2 ounces) unsweetened baking chocolate
1/3 cup margarine
1 cup sugar
2 eggs
2/3 cup all-purpose flour
1/2 teaspoon **each** baking powder and salt
1/2 cup chopped walnuts

1. Melt chocolate and margarine in double boiler insert over hot water. (Chocolate burns easily over direct heat.) Remove insert from pan of water.
2. Beat sugar and eggs into chocolate with mixing spoon.
3. Stir in remaining ingredients. Spread into greased baking pan.
4. Bake at 350ºF. for 25 minutes or until brownies are set but still moist.
5. Cool slightly before cutting. Makes about 16 brownies.

Equipment double boiler, measuring cups and spoons, mixing spoon, baking pan (8-inch square)

Chewy Butterscotch Bars

Betz's favorite. A rich, chewy cookie mixed and baked all in one pan.

1/4 cup margarine
1 cup firmly-packed brown sugar
1 egg
1 teaspoon vanilla
1/2 cup chopped walnuts
2/3 cup all-purpose flour
1 teaspoon baking powder
1/4 teaspoon salt

1. **Melt** margarine in baking pan in oven. Remove from oven. Blend in sugar, egg and vanilla with fork.
2. **Stir** in nuts, flour, baking powder and salt. Spread evenly in pan.
3. **Bake** at 350°F. for 30 minutes. Cool slightly before cutting into bars. Makes 16 cookies.

Equipment baking pan (8-inch square), measuring cups and spoons, fork

Peanut Butter Criss-Cross Cookies

1/2 cup **each** white sugar, firmly-packed brown sugar and peanut butter
1/2 cup margarine **or** butter, room temperature
1 egg
1-1/4 cups all-purpose flour
1/2 teaspoon **each** baking powder, salt and vanilla
3/4 teaspoon baking soda

1. **Combine** sugars, peanut butter, margarine and egg in mixing bowl. Mix thoroughly with mixing spoon.
2. **Add** remaining ingredients. Mix well.
3. **Roll** dough into walnut-sized balls. Place on greased baking sheet.
4. **Dip** a fork in flour and press it on each cookie twice in a criss-cross pattern, flattening the cookie by half.
5. **Bake** at 375ºF. for 10 to 12 minutes until very lightly browned. Makes about 2-1/2 dozen.

Something Different: Omit Step 4. As soon as cookies are baked press a chocolate kiss in the center of each.

 **Equipment** large mixing bowl, measuring cups and spoons, mixing spoon, baking sheet, fork

Ginger (Oatmeal) Cookies

Without the oatmeal these are thin and crisp; with oatmeal they are chewy. The aroma as they bake is reason enough to make them.

3/4 cup margarine **or** butter, at room temperature
1 cup sugar
1 egg
1/4 cup light molasses
1-1/2 cups all-purpose flour

2 teaspoons baking soda
3/4 teaspoon **each** cloves and ginger
1 teaspoon cinnamon
1/2 teaspoon salt
2 cups rolled oats (optional)

1. **Cream** butter and sugar in mixing bowl with spoon. Add egg and molasses. Beat until smooth.
2. **Stir** in remaining ingredients.
3. **Drop** dough by teaspoonfuls onto greased baking sheet about 2 inches apart.
4. **Optional** step: Dip the bottom of a glass in sugar and flatten the cookies with it to make a glaze topping.
5. **Bake** at 350°F. for 10 to 12 minutes. Cool slightly before removing from sheet with spatula. Makes about 4 dozen.

 **Equipment** large mixing bowl, measuring cups and spoons, mixing spoon, baking sheet, spatula

Campbell Cookies

1/4 cup **each** rolled oats, bran flakes, flour and instant non-fat dry milk
1/4 cup **each** sunflower seeds, chopped walnuts, shredded coconut and chopped dried apricots
3/4 cup firmly-packed brown sugar
1/4 teaspoon **each** salt, baking powder and cinnamon
1/4 cup crunchy peanut butter
2 tablespoons vegetable oil
1 egg

1. **Measure** all ingredients, in order listed, into mixing bowl. Stir until well blended.
2. **Line** baking sheet with aluminum foil. Adjust oven rack to upper third of oven. Preheat oven to 350°F.
3. **Drop** batter, the size of golf balls, onto foil. Flatten with back of spoon to form cookies 2-1/2 inch to 3 inches in diameter. Bake only 6 cookies at a time.
4. **Bake** 9 minutes, until golden brown. Let cookies cool 2 minutes, then carefully remove with spatula to plate to cool completely. Store cooled cookies in covered container. Makes 12 large cookies.

 **Equipment** large mixing bowl, measuring cups and spoons, mixing spoon, knife, baking sheet, aluminum foil, spatula

Chocolate Praline Crunch

Chewy and crunchy! An unusual combination.

2 cups corn flakes
1 cup **each** crisp rice cereal and semi-sweet chocolate chips
1 cup chopped walnuts
3/4 cup corn syrup
1/4 cup sugar
2 tablespoons margarine **or** butter
1 teaspoon vanilla

1. **Measure** cereal, chocolate chips and nuts into baking pan.
2. **Combine** remaining ingredients in saucepan and bring to a boil. Boil 3 minutes stirring constantly.
3. **Remove** from heat. Cool 10 minutes.
4. **Beat** mixture with spoon until it thickens, about 5 minutes. Pour over cereal mixture.
5. **Toss** mixture with spoon to coat evenly.
6. **Press** firmly into baking pan with fingers. Chill until set. Cut into pieces. Makes 16 large pieces.

 **Equipment** baking pan (8-inch square), measuring cups and spoons, saucepan, mixing spoon

Fudge

The best of the quick fudges.

2/3 cup (1 small can) evaporated milk
1-2/3 cups sugar
1/2 teaspoon salt
16 marshamallows, cut up **or** 2 cups miniature marshmallows
1-1/2 cups semi-sweet chocolate chips
1 teaspoon vanilla
1/2 cup chopped walnuts

1. **Combine** milk, sugar and salt in saucepan over medium heat. Bring to a boil and cook five minutes, stirring constantly.
2. **Remove** from heat. Add remaining ingredients. Stir until marshmallows melt.
3. **Pour** into buttered baking pan.
4. **Cool** and cut in squares. Makes about 40 pieces.

 **Equipment** can opener, saucepan, measuring cups and spoons, mixing spoon, knife, baking pan (8-inch square)

Almond Toffee

Making it on rainy days produces candy with unpredictable consistency, but still with delicious flavor. There are three little tricks to insure success. One . . . have all ingredients measured and ready. Two . . . watch cooking time and color of mixture closely to prevent burning. Three . . . work quickly.

1/4 cup butter **or** margarine   1/2 cup sliced or chopped almonds
1/2 cup sugar   1 cup semi-sweet chocolate chips

1. **Line** pie pan with aluminum foil. Have all ingredients measured and ready for use.
2. **Melt** butter and sugar in saucepan over medium-high heat, stirring constantly with a spoon, until sugar is melted and mixture is butter colored.
3. **Add** almonds and boil over high heat stirring constantly, 2-1/2 minutes, or less, until mixture is peanut butter colored. Remove from heat and pour immediately into foil lined pan. Quickly spread mixture evenly with the back of the spoon.
4. **Immediately** sprinkle chocolate chips over mixture. Let stand for 5 minutes while chips soften, then spread chocolate with back of spoon.
5. **Cool** about 2 hours, then break into bite-sized pieces. Store in covered container. Makes about 12 ounces.

Equipment pie pan (9-inch), measuring cups, mixing spoon. saucepan, aluminum foil

INDEX

*indicates recipe is a variation of original (found in **Something Different)**